PRICED OUT OF PARADISE

HOW TO BUILD WEALTH THROUGH REAL ESTATE IN HAWAII THE PONO WAY

KOLAIAH "FUZZY" JARDINE

Priced Out of Paradise:
How to Build Wealth Through Real Estate in Hawaii the Pono Way

Paperback: 978-1-967587-10-0
EBook: 978-1-967587-11-7

DEDICATION

Tini, I Love You. Jehovah blessed me with you as a wife along with the three beautiful keiki. Thank you for all that you do for me and our Ohana. I am proud of you, Lilinoe and Makoa, and appreciate having such respectful children. To my baby girl, Kiarah Lapeka Kekaula Jardine, I love you more than words can say. The stars are always there for you to reach. Don't ever lose sight of your dreams or ever dare to let anyone stop you from achieving them.

To all my Kanaka Maoli: You know the struggle we deal with. This is for you, if you want to make a change in your situation and create something to leave for the next generation when you are no longer here. It is our kuleana as a Kanaka Maoli to share our Mana'o and not let it get lost by keeping it to ourselves. We can teach our Lahui and do our part to keep more of us here in our homeland that we call Hawaii. This book is for those who are inside the bucket, thinking there is no way to get out. With just a little mindset shift, also known as outside-the-bucket thinking, you can achieve whatever your heart desires. For those who already got out, I encourage you to tilt the bucket and help the ones still inside to get out, too.

My heart goes out to all my Hawaiians out there who chose to move away. My hope is that this book somehow gets into your hands and gives you the motivation and inspiration to move you in the direction to someday come home to where you belong. Hawaii needs us all to stay here so we can keep the "Aloha" alive to share with the entire world and show them that it is possible to live in peace and harmony with each other. Once there are no locals in Hawaii, the Aloha will no longer be here.

Mahalo to Jehovah and Jesus his son for all the blessings in my life. Without you there would be no hope. Mom, I love you and I am forever grateful for your never-ending Aloha (love) for me. You are always there, no matter what. My Papa Alvin and Rebecca Jardine, you are missed and I owe so much to the both of you for raising me up like you did, and I am very grateful and humbled to be your Moʻopuna. Aloha and Mahalo to all of my Ohana both on my mother's side and my father's side, my two brothers and sisters, the uncles, aunties and puka panties, to all the cousins, step braddahs and sistahs. Mahalos for all the time we have spent together. Just know every one of you is always in my mind and in my heart. I can't leave out all of my best friends who have been there for me as well. You know all you hanabadah braddahs and titas, I appreciate you all being a part of the journey. Mahalo to my HUI Mastermind students for believing it is possible, and of course, Mahalo (no doubt) to my business partner, Zasha Smith, for fighting a good fight to help more locals achieve financial freedom here in Hawaii.

The choices you make today will determine your tomorrow. In other words, start doing things today that will get you where you want to be. If you choose to do or say things that set you back, then that's exactly where you will end up—"nowhere fast." If you choose to take action for your own life or outcome, not making excuses or shifting blame for where you are today, then I strongly believe you will become successful!

The people you surround yourself with help determine who you become. If you hang around with four rich people you will become the fifth!

CONTENTS

INTRODUCTION

Just because you're born in paradise doesn't mean you can afford to live there. That statement has never been more true for anyone than it is for native Hawaiians today. According to the 2020 U.S. Census, native Hawaiians make up only 23% of residents of the state of Hawaii.[1] For the first time in history, more native Hawaiians live in the continental United States than on the Hawaiian islands.[2]

A recent article in *Forbes* named Hawaii as the most expensive state to live in.[3] As the cost of living increases, the amount of disposable income available to help locals make ends meet, shrinks. This means it becomes harder and harder for Hawaiians to get ahead.

Just how alarming are the numbers? How about this one: The average price for a single family home in Hawaii was $982,800 in 2022, with tourist areas being even higher.[4] It's no wonder around 15,000 native Hawaiians leave the state for the continent every year![5]

Hawaiians are being priced out of paradise, and it's time for something to change. It's time to start taking a different path forward!

From Ex-Con to Real Estate Investor

At this point, you might be wondering about the person writing this book. Hi, my name is Kolaiah Jardine, but my friends call me Fuzzy. I'm a father, a proud native Hawaiian, and a successful real estate investor. My journey to real estate investing wasn't typical, but I think that's a good thing, and I'll tell you why. But first, let me tell you a little bit about my journey.

I grew up with nothing, and my family worked hard just to survive. I always knew I wanted more, but that desire for more got me in trouble early on. I fell in with the wrong crowd, started selling drugs, and ended up in prison. It was during my time there that I turned my back on my former way of life. I chose to take a new, upright path—a path that helped me build generational wealth for my Ohana and provide affordable housing for other native Hawaiians. I'll describe what that path looked like a little further on in this book. For now, just know that my journey wasn't easy, but for you, that's good news.

Because if a regular guy, who came from nothing, got mixed up with the wrong crowd, and ended up in prison, can become a real estate investor and change his entire Ohana's financial legacy, you can too.

Even with the harsh statistics I just listed, Hawaiians still have options when it comes to taking control of their time and income to preserve and uphold their way of life here in Hawaii.

I'm convinced real estate investing is one of the best options out there, and I'm on a mission to help native Hawaiians learn how to get started the RIGHT way—the Pono Way.

ABOUT THIS BOOK

With a strong reason "why" that will motivate and keep you focused, you can do anything you put your mind to. In this book, I'm going to show that you CAN invest in real estate, and I'm going to give you the practical, step-by-step framework to do so.

The best part about this whole process is once you know what to do, you can get started with just two things:

- OPT – Other people's time
- OPM – Other people's money

As you read through this book, you'll learn the simple steps to get started with real estate investing so that you can build confidence by learning exactly what to do. This is the book I wish I'd had when I first started.

As I think back, my own story of getting into real estate began when I heard about this specific kind of investing from another inmate while I was still in prison. Although I had a chance to read books and take classes while I was incarcerated, I had zero dollars to my name and no idea where to start once I got out.

Once I was out of prison, I looked for ways to learn about real estate investing in our community, but it took me a long time to find anything. Most people in Hawaii who were involved in real estate investment weren't sharing their secrets, as if there weren't enough deals to go around.

That couldn't be further from the truth. Deals are EVERYWHERE, and in this book, you'll discover that unlike the community members I looked to for help (the ones who kept all their knowledge to themselves), I don't hold back when it comes to giving you the information you need. I share it all!

But this is more than just a "how to become a real estate investor" book.

This is also a book about helping native Hawaiians break out of old patterns and get inspired to take a new path. The reality is you don't have to give all your time to growing someone else's business. You're not going to hear this from your family and friends, though, so let me be the first to tell you that you can have your OWN real estate investing business.

And if you're from Hawaii and want to invest in Hawaiian properties, this book will be useful for you, too. Hawaiian life and culture can endure and flourish with your help. This book will help you catch the vision for investing in a way that preserves the Pono Way—a way of living that leads with love and integrity and puts others ahead of yourself.

WHAT THIS BOOK WILL DO FOR YOU

By the time you finish reading this book, you'll have certainty in your ability to become a real estate investor in Hawaii. You'll believe you can build generational wealth that leaves a legacy for your children and your children's children. And you'll know you can do it all while being a part of helping preserve Hawaii's unique culture and history.

Real estate investment has enabled me to do all of that and more. I grew up with nothing, and my Ohana worked hard just to survive. Real estate investing freed me from the rut I was stuck in and made it possible for me to generate the income I need to stay in Hawaii where I belong.

Today, I manage a multimillion-dollar real estate portfolio. I bought my mother a house in 2022, and I've been able to keep our Ohana land preserved for us when it would have otherwise been lost to outsiders. I have also helped dozens of other families obtain home ownership at affordable prices in Hawaii.

And you know what else? What I've been able to do in real estate has given me my time back. As you read these words, my real estate investing business is running without me physically having to operate it. How? Because of the systems I have put into place. Systems you will learn about inside this book.

All of that is great, but what means the most to me is having been able to help dozens of Hawaiians find success as real estate investors inside the Hawaii Ultimate Investor (HUI) Academy and Mastermind program, which is run by my business partner, Zasha Smith, and me.

Whether you're looking to do this full time or as a side hustle, this book is your blueprint to getting started in real estate investing. If you're ready for education, accountability, and coaching from boots-on-the-ground investors like Zasha and me, visit https://huimastermind.com/case-study-3-ways-to-start to learn more about the HUI Mastermind and to book a chat.

Now let's dive into chapter one so I can show you how YOU are the answer Hawaii real estate needs today.

Aloha!

Fuzzy

PART 1

The Pono Way

Chapter 1

Hawaii Real Estate Needs You

I'm not proud of the choices I made as a younger man. I told you I was entrepreneurial, but what I didn't tell you was not all of my entrepreneurial pursuits were aboveboard. I started following the wrong crowds, adopted the wrong kind of lifestyle, and got into selling drugs. That's how I ended up in prison.

Thankfully, prison was the wake-up call I needed. Right away, I decided prison would not be the end of my story. I made the most of every opportunity to better myself while I was inside. I took classes and learned about all kinds of business opportunities while I was there. For the first time, my mind was opened to the idea that there were other options to make money besides working for someone else or selling drugs to survive in Hawaii. Prison was actually the place where I first became interested in real estate investing after hearing about it from another inmate who was serving time for tax evasion.

But being interested in it and doing something about it are two different things, right?

I also did a lot of personal development while I was inside. I read Robert Kiyosaki's *Rich Dad Poor Dad*, Napoleon Hill's *Keys to Success*, Tony Robbins' *Awaken the Giant Within*, and Dale Carnegie's *How to Win Friends and Influence People*. I made a vow that upon release, I'd never end up back in prison again. I would do whatever it took to create a better future for myself and for my family.

LIFE ON THE OUTSIDE

In 2007, I was released from prison and started getting back on my feet, but transitioning back into a normal life on the outside wasn't easy. My dreams of investing in real estate seemed impossible. I didn't know the first thing about getting started, so one of the first things I did after getting out of prison was to look for a job. That was the only way I thought I could make a living, but finding a good job as an ex-con was *hard*.

I applied for every position I could find, but nobody wanted to hire someone with a record. Door after door was slammed in my face. I wanted to be a car salesman because I knew that selling cars would put money in my pocket pretty quickly. But every car dealership refused to hire me. Thankfully, I had a buddy who got me a job as a window washer, but it was going to take a lot more than working as a window washer to create the kind of future I was dreaming of.

I added another job, and then another. Eventually, I was holding down three jobs working for other people instead of myself. I spent hours a day commuting from job to job, and it was getting old. It was time to put wheels on my idea of having my own business.

I had a buddy who was making over $100,000 a year as a pilot. I figured if I could get my pilot's license, I could do that, too. I went to the bank and got a $20,000 educational loan from the OHA Mālama Loan Program so I could afford to go to school to get my pilot's license. But God had other plans for me. On the way home, I heard an ad on my car radio that changed everything.

The ad promoted a free event where people could learn about real estate investing, and it caught my attention. *Maybe this free event can help*, I thought.

I signed up, went, and spent two hours learning about how people buy houses, fix them up, and sell them for a profit—all without ever using their own money. If that was true, it could be exactly the strategy I needed to change my Ohana's future. At the time, I was dating the woman who would later become my wife, and I told her, "I know they're going to try to sell me something, but I just have to see what this is all about."

During the free seminar, they promoted a three-day event for $197 where you could come and hear more. I was in! What I learned during that event made everything click. The best part was the speaker was a surfer guy just like me— with a family. I remember thinking that if he could become a real estate investor, so could I.

Long story short, I never became a pilot. Instead, I used the $20,000 education loan and a credit card to join a $26,000 coaching program called FortuneBuilders so I could learn everything I needed to know to start investing in real estate in my own backyard.

Making that investment in my education changed my life and the lives of everyone in my Ohana. Today, I know it was no accident that I heard that exact ad at that exact moment in my life, and now, I also know it wasn't just for me and my family. It was so I could be here today, writing this book to show you how, if I can do it, you can do it, too.

MY PURPOSE AS A HAWAII REAL ESTATE INVESTOR

I took what I learned from my coaches inside FortuneBuilders and looked at it all through the lens of how it could apply to Hawaii real estate. But I took things a level further, thinking about how I could use that information to help Hawaiians and locals. I didn't want to become just another investor who came in, bought up land, and made life harder for the people who already live here.

And honestly, I wasn't an overnight success as a real estate investor. It takes a lot of work to become any kind of investor. I didn't even know what I didn't know in the beginning. Plus, I didn't really have any money of my own to invest at first, not the kind you need in the Hawaii real estate market. I learned as I went along, though, picking up helpful skills and making myself indispensable to my coaches. Sometimes I worked hours upon hours for free so I could learn what they knew about real estate investing.

I wore any hat they needed me to, just so I could work with them. I acted as a construction guy, marketing specialist, project manager, and deal finder. And the first deal I found was really close to home—my Ohana's house. When I first got out of prison, my mom and stepdad let me stay in their house while I got back on my feet. Now, their home was in foreclosure, so I went straight to the real estate coaches who were teaching me for help.

My coaches walked me through what an investor would do in that situation, and they took the time to drive to my family's house. They gave my parents some options and offered to help them out of their foreclosure situation, letting them know that it wasn't going to be an easy solution.

Not only did my mom and stepdad live in the house, my brother, sister, and their partners were all living there, too. If they sold the house, where would everyone go? Multiple families living together in one home is a really common situation in Hawaii.

From 2021 to 2022 alone—foreclosures rose 94%![5] As more and more native Hawaiians fall into foreclosure, they can't afford to stay and are forced to leave their homeland, which is heartbreaking.

Eventually, my brother stepped up and helped to pay the mortgage while my parents got back on their feet. My Ohana's home was saved, but that's not the case for everyone. I realized my purpose as a real estate investor was to make a difference for my people the Pono Way—from the heart. I wanted to improve my Ohana's financial future for sure, but I also wanted to empower all Hawaiians by providing options that would make it possible for them and their children to continue to live in their homelands.

That desire was about to be put to the test with my first real project.

THE BEST $12,000 I EVER MADE

Because I didn't have any of my own money to invest—and as you read this book, you'll learn having your own capital up front isn't necessary—another student in the coaching program I was in presented me with my first opportunity. The project was owned by an older lady with no ohana who was in distress and couldn't pay her mortgage. This woman would have lost her property to sharks if the other student— my partner—hadn't stepped in to see what was happening with her situation. The home was in Kailua Kona, Hawaii. A single woman was living in a house that was too large, and she couldn't keep up with the mortgage payments.

The other student and I took over the woman's mortgage payments (you'll learn more about how we did that later in this book), but we didn't just turn her out with zero options. We gave her money upfront and on the back end of the deal, too. We put her up in an apartment, paid six months' rent for her, and got her a new car. Our coaches put up their own personal money and we leveraged hard money from the FortuneBuilders to fix up the home. Then, we put it back on the market and sold it. Because of the way we structured this deal, she was able to get out from under the mortgage of her too-big home and stay in Hawaii.

In one project, I learned so much! I learned how to find

deals with others, how to fund deals with other people's money and hard money, how to build a creative solution that took care of the property owner, and how to manage the project alongside the other student.

In the end, EVERYONE profited—my project partner and I, our coaches, and the original homeowner. I made $12,000, and I'll never forget how good it felt to realize I'd been part of a real solution that created a positive outcome for all doing it the PONO WAY!

WHAT'S HAPPENING TODAY?

It's been about ten years since my first deal, and writing this book, I no longer work three jobs helping grow other people's businesses. I have my own real estate investing company! Deal by deal, I've grown a multimillion-dollar real estate portfolio, and I've hired a team to help.

I also have control of my own time in a way I would have never experienced as an employee. I don't have to give all my hours to help grow someone else's business. There's no more three-hour commute. No more working multiple jobs while never really getting ahead.

My wife, children, and I have the freedom to do what we want, when we want. We can travel. We homeschool our youngest daughter. And best of all, we can afford to stay on the islands, living in our own piece of paradise.

Real estate investing has enabled me to create generational wealth so my children, my grandchildren, and all our future descendants will benefit. I've also been able to get into more advanced strategies not covered in this book, like infinite banking and using whole life insurance policies to fund projects and protect my family.

But the thing I'm most proud of today is that I now teach others how to ethically invest in Hawaii real estate through my HUI Mastermind Academy and HUI Mastermind.

I don't just talk about how great real estate investing is. I pull back the curtain and reveal how ANYONE who wants to can do it. I share everything about what to do and how to get started using other people's money and other people's time.

DOES THIS REALLY WORK?

Hawaii real estate investing is a great way to make money, but you don't have to take my word for it. Let's just look at the facts about real estate investing. According to *Investopedia*, real estate investing can provide passive income and stable cash flow.[1] When you have income that doesn't rely on personal sweat equity, what does that mean? For many Hawaiians, having access to this kind of income would change their lives!

All investing comes with an element of risk, but real estate is one of the safest investments you can make. It's not subject to inflation the same way the rest of the economy is. In fact, rent prices often increase with inflation, so if you're into rentals, your income could rise over time.[3]

And don't forget about appreciation, the way property tends to increase in value over time. Hawaii homes have always appreciated well over time.[4] Plus, when you make improvements to a property, you actually increase the property's value, which can lead to higher sales or rental prices.[2] And did I mention the tax benefits? You can use mortgage interest and other real estate costs as tax deductions.[3]

DON'T WORRY, I'M NOT SPECIAL

Now before you start thinking things like, "That's great for you, Fuzzy, but I'm not you. I could never do that," here's what you need to know: It doesn't just work for me. It can work for anyone whose "why" is strong, who gets the right training and mentorship, and is willing to work hard. Here are some real-life stories of students who have used the framework I teach inside HUI Academy and Mastermind.

Brandan and Tom

For example, take my students Brandan and Tom. I met Brandan, a wedding photographer, at a trade show several years ago. He followed me on social media for years. Then one day, he saw one of my posts about real estate investing and sent me a direct message. We set up a meeting to see if we could partner on a brand-new build. He was curious about what I was doing, and he wanted to learn.

I started teaching Brandan real estate investing, and his friend Tom, an electrician, joined us. It didn't take them long to jump in with both feet and go in with me on their first deal. They provided the funding to buy land, and my team built a new house on it.

We then sold the new home to a single mom for $350,000. Most homes in Hawaii that size would cost THREE TIMES as much, and that home changed her life. It gave her a place where she and her kids could afford to live, and that was something she never thought she'd have. Not only that, it changed Brandan and Tom's lives, too. Once they saw how real estate investing not only made them a profit but helped another Hawaiian family, they were hooked.

Right away, Brandan went out and got more funding. He bought 17 lots and we built affordable homes on all of them. Today, Brandan and Tom have created an amazing real estate investing business. They took what I taught them, put it to work, and in 2025, they had 60+ projects going on their own!

Both men are now living at a higher level of financial success, and Tom only does electrical work on the side. They didn't just learn, they took action. They started investing in real estate the Pono Way, and now dozens of families have homes they can afford right here in their homeland.

Skyler

Then there's Skyler, a 26-year-old who found my business partner, Zasha Smith, and me on social media. He watched our videos, read books on real estate investing, and took part in one of our workshops. He didn't have any money of his own to invest with, but he was determined to make something work.

Skyler put together a presentation with research, numbers, and everything. Then he pitched the idea of taking out a home equity line of credit to his parents. After some convincing, his parents agreed, and that's how he funded his first deal.

Skyler purchased a lot and closed a deal on a new build—using none of his own money—and made $120,000. Now he's working on his second and third projects, still without using any of his own money to fund them.

Keola

And finally, there's Keola. Keola is one of six siblings raised by a single mom. Thirty-five years into his career as a schoolteacher, he decided to look into real estate investing as a way to secure his future. He had taken a real estate investing course with a big-name "guru" in the past, but he struggled to put what he learned to work in the Hawaii real estate market.

When Keola heard about HUI Mastermind, he knew he had found the missing piece. He joined the HUI Mastermind in February 2024 and began implementing everything we teach inside the program right away.

He used the HUI Framework to raise capital, purchase a lot, and start a brand-new build. By Father's Day of the same year, he had purchased his second property, with plans to repeat the process. At the writing of this book, he had plans to submit a third offer. Keola is well on his way to financial freedom that doesn't rely on his nine-to-five job!

These stories feature people who didn't have a real estate background or their own money when they got started, yet they were able to take what they learned inside HUI Academy and Mastermind to create their own results.

If they can do it—heck, if *I* can do it—you can do it, too! Real estate investing can give you the ability to stop trading your time for money while working to grow other people's businesses. It can help you break out of the rut you're in and start building something that's YOURS. Something that can set your family up for life by creating generational wealth like I have!

INVESTING IN REAL ESTATE THE PONO WAY

When I first started investing in real estate, I knew how much I needed it. If I was ever going to change my family's financial legacy, I needed a new way to generate income that wasn't dependent on my own money or time.

What I didn't realize was how much Hawaii real estate also needed *me*. And it needs you, too. Deals are everywhere. Unfortunately, not all deals fall into the right hands. I could tell you story after story about outside investors who come in, buy real estate, and build multimillion-dollar mansions that sit empty for months on end. Mansions that are unaffordable to native Hawaiians who need places to live.

We need more native Hawaii real estate investors and mainland real estate investors who are willing to invest the Pono Way so Hawaiians can find affordable housing that allows them to stay in their homeland.

What is the Pono Way? Pono is a Hawaiian term that means "righteousness." If you're a native Hawaiian reading this book right now, you know that when you do something the Pono Way, you do what's right even when no one is looking. When you invest in real estate the Pono Way, you invest respectfully, looking out for more than just your own financial gain.

The truth is, investing in Hawaii real estate is different than investing in real estate anywhere else. There are unique cultural, societal, and geographic challenges and benefits to investing here that aren't present elsewhere. And that means you need to have a different approach, so everyone comes out on top.

There's a right way and a wrong way to invest in Hawaii real estate, and in this book, you're going to learn the Pono Way—the HUI Framework way. There's no better, faster way to get where you want to be than to learn from someone who's already been there and done that. That someone is me, and this book can be the guide you need to start taking action and change your life.

HERE'S WHAT'S COMING UP...

In part 1 of this book, you will learn more about whether you'd be a good investor in Hawaii real estate. Plus, I'll explain how you can avoid the pitfalls and challenges other investors have fallen into.

In part 2, I break down the HUI Framework step-by-step, so you know exactly what to do to start investing the Pono Way—and all without having to use your own money or time.

Part 3 will talk about why Hawaii is one of the best places to invest in real estate right now. I also describe some of the challenges investors face when it comes to Hawaii real estate and how to deal with those potential issues.

Finally, part 4 will give you a shortcut to getting started. It's a planning exercise I share with all my HUI Academy and Mastermind students. This exercise will help you get clear on your "why" and give you a step-by-step blueprint so that you know the first steps to take when you invest in Hawaii real estate.

As you continue reading, think about this: where your focus goes, your energy flows. Don't ignore the opportunities in front of you, ones that will further your family and your dream of having your own business.

MAIN TAKEAWAYS FROM CHAPTER 1

1. **If I can do it, you can, too.** I didn't come from money. I spent time in prison and started from the bottom when I got out. I didn't have a job, and I didn't know how I was going to turn my life around. I just knew I was going to. One radio ad about real estate investing changed everything for me. That was the beginning of the journey that led me to build a multimillion-dollar portfolio. And I'm not special—if I can do it, so can you.

2. **Real estate can save families—mine is proof!** The first deal I ever looked into wasn't some random house. It was my own family's house that was in foreclosure. I realized real estate investing could be the solution that so many families need. It's about helping people—starting with your own ohana or Hawaiian brothers and sisters. That situation lit a fire in me to help other Hawaiians protect what's theirs.

3. **You don't need your own money to get started. You just need the right knowledge.** I didn't have $26,000 to invest in coaching, but I found a way because I was willing to sacrifice and do whatever it took. The truth is you don't need your own cash to start investing in Hawaii real estate. You just need the education and a willingness to hustle. That's what I did, and that's what I teach inside the HUI Mastermind.

4. **The Pono Way is the BEST way to invest in real estate in Hawaii.** There's a right way and a wrong way to invest in real estate in Hawaii, and I'm here to teach you the right way—the Pono Way. That means doing deals that help the people, protect the land, and make Hawaii better for the next generation. This way, there is purpose *and* profit!

Chapter 2

Hello, Future Hawaii Real Estate Investor!

For as long as I can remember, I've been entrepreneurial-minded. I wanted to have my own business and be my own boss. But when you grow up poor like I did, living in Hawaii meant there weren't a lot of options for bettering your circumstances.

So, I did what I could. I started out young as a paperboy and next, I became a bag boy at a grocery store. Then, I pumped gas at a gas station. After that, I worked my way from dishwasher to server at a restaurant. In high school, my uncle got me into selling Amway, and I had my own downline selling products. I worked as a baggage handler at the airport. I bought, flipped, and sold cars. I was even in the Army Reserve for a while.

I spent years working for other people, helping them grow their businesses. For someone who values freedom and desperately wanted to help his family escape the poverty they were in, this was frustrating. I wanted out of the cycle of poverty, but escape wasn't easy.

THE CRAB IN THE BUCKET

Hawaii is home to the *a'ama*, a species of black crab that hides among the black rocks on the coastline. This small crab is a popular source of bait and food for natives and island visitors. They move really fast, so you have to go out and catch them at night by hand, then put them in a bucket to take them home.

Once a crab gets tossed into the bucket with other crabs, it's almost impossible for it to get out. Even if the bucket is so full that a crab could hook a pincer over the lip to pull itself out, the other crabs will grab the escapee and pull it back into the bucket.

That's how it feels trying to get ahead and break the cycle of poverty in Hawaii sometimes. You try to better yourself and make it out of the bucket, but the people around you don't understand why. They mean well, but they only know the way of life they've had, and that's the life they expect you to lead, too. They're afraid of what you could become if you launch out into uncharted waters because they've seen the negative impact, like when high maka maka people come in and buy up the land without caring for the people. They don't want that to happen to you, so they pull you back in.

The crab in the bucket mentality led me to make some really bad decisions. Even though I wanted to rise above my circumstances and make something of myself, my family and friends didn't get it. I surrounded myself with people who offered me an "in" on the only life they knew—selling drugs. But it was a life that would only put me on a path to prison.

HOW I TILTED THE BUCKET

As you can see from this book, I made it out. I got out of prison, put in the work to educate myself, and took action by investing in real estate here in Hawaii. Now I teach other Hawaiians how to do the same thing. But there are so many Hawaiians still stuck in the bucket, getting dragged down into a dead-end future because they choose to listen to family and friends who tell them not to go for it or who fear what others think or would say about them.

There aren't many options for Hawaiians without a college degree who don't want to work minimum wage for someone else their whole lives. According to a 2022 report, the top four job categories on the islands include office and administrative support, tourism and food service, retail sales, and transportation and moving services, all of which average less than $50,000 per year.[1] The average price of homes in Hawaii is almost $1,000,000![2] Anyone with basic math skills can see the numbers don't work out in the favor of native Hawaiians.

And honestly, I don't blame those who are from here for not wanting to put themselves in that position. They won't be able to afford to buy a home unless they work two or three jobs, and there goes all their time and freedom. I know, because that's how I lived for years until I got into real estate investing.

To many, it feels like they're priced right out of paradise because of the high cost of living and high property values. They desperately want to break the cycle their families have been in for generations. Each of them wants to be the one who makes it, the one who becomes the first millionaire in their family—but how? It's tricky to pin down an answer.

WHO THIS BOOK IS FOR

This book was written with three types of people in mind, and the lessons and information inside can change the lives of all three kinds.

First, this book is for someone who relates to the crab in the bucket story. You love your family and friends, but you don't have the same dreams they do. You dream of a bigger future where your time is your own and you're financially free. And not just for today—you want to create the kind of wealth that will leave a legacy and impact your family for generations. If that describes you, investing in Hawaii real estate could be your escape route! Keep reading so you can learn how to get started using other people's money and other people's time.

This book is for the native Hawaiian who has been priced out of the real estate market. Maybe you live on the mainland or in a foreign country now because you can no longer afford the high cost of living in Hawaii. Great news— investing in Hawaii real estate could be your ticket back home. After all, if investors from the mainland can benefit from the Hawaii real estate market, why not you? Keep reading to learn how Hawaii real estate investors are helping improve quality of life for Hawaiians and how you can get involved.

Finally, maybe you're someone who isn't Hawaiian at all, but loves Hawaii and its people. You're fascinated with the idea of getting started investing in Hawaii real estate, and you want to do it the Pono Way so Hawaiian culture and the land are preserved and everyone benefits. Well, then this book is for you, too. Keep reading so you can learn the ins and outs of Hawaii real estate investing. It's different from investing in any other market in the world.

HERE'S WHAT I'M REALLY TEACHING YOU IN THIS BOOK...

This book will teach you how to invest in Hawaii real estate the Pono Way using the HUI Framework. But on a deeper level, this book is the blueprint for taking control of your life, your time, and your finances so you can be the crab who makes it out of the bucket, then reaches back in and helps others get out, too.

If you're one of the three types of people I've written this book for, the most powerful thing you can do for yourself right now is to start dreaming about what your life could look like as a real estate investor. Instead of investing in things that lose value over time, why not learn how to invest in real estate, which appreciates in value over time? This book will show you how to get started and what to do every step of the way.

Most importantly, stop procrastinating and telling yourself, "I'll start tomorrow." Start today. Right now. You don't have to work three jobs and miss holidays, special events, or birthdays with your kids. You don't have to spend your life working to grow someone else's business. Grow your own!

Whatever you do, don't still be in the same spot a year from now. Let's do this together, future Hawaii real estate investor!

MAIN TAKEAWAYS FROM CHAPTER 2

1. **The crab in the bucket mentality is real.** In Hawaii, when you try to do something different—especially something that looks like success—people around you can get nervous. They'll call you high maka maka or try to pull you back because they're scared of change. I've been there. But if we want to break generational cycles and build real wealth, someone's gotta be the first to reach for the edge of the bucket. Why not you?

2. **Real estate investing helped me tilt the bucket and get out.** Growing up in Hawaii without a college degree or a lot of options, I used to feel like the only way to survive was to work multiple low-paying jobs. I did that for years—grinding, commuting, barely making it. But that wasn't the future I wanted for myself or my family. Real estate investing gave me the chance to take control of my time and income. It was the thing that helped me finally tip the bucket and climb out.

3. **Hawaiians don't have to leave home to build wealth.** So many locals think the only way to afford a good life is to move to the mainland. I don't believe that has to be true. Real estate investing—done the Pono Way—can give us a way to stay here, build wealth, and keep our families rooted in Hawaii. If outsiders can come here and make money off our land, we can do it, too—with heart, respect, and purpose.

4. **This book is for the crab who wants out.** Whether you're a local trying to break free, a Hawaiian living on the mainland who wants to come home, or a mainlander who wants to invest in real estate in Hawaii the right way—this book is for you. I'm not just teaching real estate. I'm teaching you how to take your life back, make your own rules, and reach back in to help others out of the bucket once you've made it.

Chapter 3

Why Is This So Hard?

I f you read the first two chapters of this book, and right now you're thinking, "That sounds great for you Fuzzy, but..." that's okay. I get it. I've been in real estate investing for 12 years now, but I still remember what it was like getting started. I knew without a doubt that this was my path and it was time to take action, but I had a hard time finding people I could learn from, so I had questions, too.

Lucky for you, you don't have to go in blind. You're in the right place because this is the part of the book where I'm going to reveal exactly what's keeping Hawaiians and mainlanders from getting started and how the HUI Framework can help.

But first, let me tell you something, so we're on the same page. I'm not saying that real estate investing is an easy pushbutton to make money. It takes action and hard work, and I sure made my share of mistakes along the way. However, when you know where to start and what to do at each step, you realize that it's actually quite simple.

Okay, now that we have that settled, let's dive into the rest of the chapter. Let's get your questions answered so you can move forward with your real estate investing dreams with confidence. Let's start with the issues native Hawaiians are concerned about—ones that hold them back before they initially get into real estate investing.

NATIVE HAWAIIAN CONCERNS ABOUT REAL ESTATE INVESTING IN HAWAII

"I want to be the crab that makes it out of the bucket, but won't people think I'm high maka maka?"

Hawaiians use the phrase "high maka maka" to describe someone who thinks they're better than others—and they don't mean it as a compliment.

What's different or new is often feared. Things that are familiar feel safe. Seeing you dive in can be scary for a friend or family member who doesn't understand real estate investing. Real estate investing isn't a traditional path for a Hawaiian, so sometimes the people around you, like your family, friends, or coworkers, will try to discourage you from going for it. It's that same "crab in the bucket" mentality I talked about in the last chapter. They don't mean to pull you back, but they are scared for you to choose something that is not what they are used to.

This happens a lot when you come from a blue-collar background where positions or trades are passed down from generation to generation. Many Hawaiians have only ever known working for someone else their whole lives. Doing something different doesn't seem safe, and to them, your choice of a different path might seem like a slap in the face to the traditional way of life they follow. But just because someone doesn't understand your dream doesn't mean you're becoming high maka maka!

Having money isn't a bad thing if you have a good heart. Money can amplify the kind of person you already are. Are there some real estate investors who come to Hawaii and take advantage of Hawaiians for their own gain, then go sit in their mansions looking down on others? Sure, but if that's the kind of attitude they have, it was likely in their heart before they ever made the money.

You're different. If you have good, or Aloha, in your heart and want to become a real estate investor to better your life, support your family, and build a legacy while helping other Hawaiians, great! Your positive qualities will only increase with success. You'll have a greater capacity for doing good, and the good you do will be amplified so you can become part of the positive change needed for Hawaii and its future generations.

"I never even went to college, and I don't know anything about real estate investing. Is succeeding in this industry even possible for me?"

I never went to college either. I went to prison. Honestly, you really only need two things to succeed in real estate investing:

1. **Education.** First, learn what to do and how to do it from someone who's already doing it. You don't need a college degree.

2. **Action.** Then, you actually do what you've learned in the form of action.

It's really that simple. As long as you can learn and have the ability to take action, you can get started now...and you have, just by starting to read this book!

There are tons of great ways to learn about real estate investing. If you have a smartphone, you can start Googling or searching YouTube for information from the palm of your hand—then take action. Or you could enroll in a course or coaching program, like my HUI Academy and Mastermind. When you learn from people who have walked the path before you, you can go faster with fewer mistakes.

And when I say faster, I mean it. We have a student in the HUI Mastermind right now named Maile. She only joined a few months ago, and she's already done her first project. I like to go out and find deals, make offers, and get a contract started, then drop them in the community for the students to take action on. They can partner up with each other and work together to get funding and do the deals. Maile partnered up with Keola, who you read about in chapter one, and now they're doing a brand-new build on the Big Island.

The nice thing about enrolling in a course or coaching program is you can get a step-by-step blueprint to real estate investing in Hawaii from start to finish, plus support from the coaches and other students. More than 100 students have taken the opportunity to change their lives and learn real estate, investing the Pono Way with me and my business partner, Zasha Smith.

However you decide to learn and take action: Make the decision that you're done settling for less in life. You CAN do better, and the truth is, YOU are the only one stopping you. Instead of being afraid of failure, learn to be afraid of things never changing.

"Hawaii is one of the most expensive real estate markets out there. Where am I going to find the money to buy property?"

Where there's a will, there's a way. Think about the last thing you really, really wanted. You figured out how to get it, right? The great thing about real estate investing is you don't need your own money to do it. You can leverage credit, equity in your home, or find investors.

When I first started out, I wanted to join a coaching program called FortuneBuilders. I knew I needed help learning how to become a real estate investor, but the program cost $26,000. Did I have $26,000 lying around? Nope. But I had access to credit. I could have used my credit for something else, like a fancy truck with a lift kit and titanium rims. Those are nice, right?

The problem with buying something like a truck is the minute you drive it off the lot, it depreciates in value. It's worth thousands less almost instantly. Property, on the other hand, appreciates over time and has the power to generate passive income for you in the form of rental payments.

I used my credit to pay for the education I needed because I knew that I could leverage that credit to get the result I wanted. That credit helped me invest in an asset that appreciates and pays out in passive income over time.

By practicing delayed gratification, I was able to build assets in the form of rentals that pay for my liabilities. Everyone around me had gold chains, Harley-Davidsons, and Toyota Tacomas with fancy rims. That was not for me. I decided to live a more humble life so I could put the money towards real estate investing to help the local community have more affordable housing. The passive income I make allows me to keep investing over and over again. It's worth waiting on some of the new, shiny stuff to be able to build wealth for the future.

Plus there are lots of resources out there that can help you get your finances in order so that you're ready to invest. One of them is the self-assessment at the end of this chapter. I also recommend the resources below. (Check the Resources section of this book for links.)

- **Hawaiian Community Assets** is a nonprofit organization that offers free financial education and information on grants and loans that can help Hawaiians build generational wealth they can pass onto future generations.
- **Hawai'i Community Lending** is another nonprofit organization that lends to local businesses. It also connects people with federal grants and low-interest nonprofit funds that are offered at a few percentage points of interest. Any entity set up as an LLC with a profit and loss statement can apply for a line of credit. That's what I did. There was a brand-new building project I

needed funding for. I applied for and received a line of credit at 5–6% to fund some new builds.

- **101 Financial** is another great resource that provides paid financial counseling and resources for Hawaiians. If you go to their website, you can even download the digital version of *The Super Duper Simple Book on Money* by Alan Akina, CEO of 101 Financial.

"I don't have support or anyone to ask when I have questions. Who can I turn to for help?"

Do you know why Zasha and I named our program the HUI Mastermind? HUI is an acronym that stands for Hawaii Ultimate Investor, but that's not the only reason we gave it that name. Hui is also a Hawaiian word that means unity or community, and that's what we are inside the Mastermind. We're a united community, like a family, that lifts each other up and creates opportunities for partnering on deals.

With this book in your hands, you're getting a glimpse of the kind of information and education our mastermind students have access to. But, as you take this journey, it's up to you to surround yourself with the right kind of people who can support you as you grow.

When I was in prison, I had a choice. I could have surrounded myself with the same kind of people I'd been hanging out with—people like the ones who introduced me to drugs and put me on the path that led to incarceration. And you know what? Nothing would have changed. I would have gotten out no better off than when I'd gone in. I didn't want that. I didn't want to go back to the same habits and behaviors that put me in prison.

Instead, I took every opportunity I could find to sit with people who could teach me things that would help me better myself. I asked questions and studied and learned. Bottom line, if I could find a way to surround myself with the right people even from prison, you can find a way to surround yourself with the right people, too!

CONCERNS FROM MAINLANDERS AND HAWAIIANS WHO LIVE ON THE MAINLAND

Investing in Hawaii real estate isn't just for Hawaiians who live on the islands. In fact, you don't even have to be Hawaiian to invest in real estate in Hawaii.

Maybe you're reading this book right now because you're a Hawaiian living on the mainland looking for a way to come back home. You see mainlanders investing in real estate all around you, and it's got you thinking that maybe real estate investing can help make it possible to move your family back to the islands. Well, you're thinking right!

Or maybe you're not Hawaiian. Maybe you're a real estate investor who recognizes the unique opportunity the Hawaii real estate market offers, and you want to get involved. The rest of this chapter is for you.

"How do I break into real estate investing in Hawaii? I know it's not the same as investing in the mainland."

The Hawaii real estate market is different—that is for sure. Not only is it an expensive real estate market, there are a lot of cultural and geographical concerns to be aware of. For example, the Hawaiian Islands are actually a chain of volcanoes. It's important to be familiar with where things like lava tubes are so you're not building a project on top of a future problem. Land ownership and deeds can also be tricky in Hawaii due to kuleana lands and the Bishop Estate, things we'll talk about more in part 3 of this book. If you try to break into real estate investing in Hawaii using the best practices that work on the mainland, you'll struggle.

The good news is this book will give you a step-by-step blueprint to real estate investing in Hawaii from start to finish using the Pono Way and the HUI Framework. The HUI Framework is the only framework I've ever seen that includes real estate investment training PLUS training specific to investing the Pono Way, which includes a heartfelt desire to help further Hawaii, its people, and its culture.

There may be real estate investing coaches out there who are better marketers with bigger budgets, but they don't have the heart or the background we do. I grew up here on the Islands. Both Zasha and I came from nothing, and we know what it's like to want something different, something bigger. We also know all the ins and outs of the Hawaii real estate market, the nuances of owning property depending on which island you purchase or develop real estate, and how to do deals in a way that honors culture and tradition.

I'm pouring my heart into this book because Zasha and I want to help the next Zasha and Fuzzy crawl out of the bucket. We want to make it possible for more Hawaiians to change their lives with real estate investing in a way that also provides affordable homes for more Hawaiians.

"I don't know all the unique ins and outs of owning property in Hawaii. What do I need to be aware of?"

Owning property in Hawaii is definitely different from what you might expect on the mainland. For example, we have what's called kuleana lands, which are lands given to native Hawaiians by the kings. Unfortunately over time, many natives lost their rights or didn't know how to claim them, leaving the question of who owns what up in the air. This has led to a lot of legal battles today, and that can get tricky for investors.

Then there's the additional challenge caused by the Bishop Estate, one of the largest and wealthiest trusts in the world. The trust manages land for the Kamehameha Schools as well as a large portion of land that's under long-term leasehold.

Under long-term leasehold arrangements, people or businesses can buy structures, like a house or building, but they don't actually own the land—it's leased, sometimes for up to one hundred years. At the end of that lease, it goes back to the state unless the leasee buys out the fee simple rights (which I'll explain more about later in the book). This can be a real surprise for people new to investing here.

And don't forget the environmental considerations— lava zones, landlocked properties (land impossible to access without going onto the land of others), and oceanfront regulations can all affect what you can do with your land. In 2023, we saw firsthand the impact Hawaii's unique geography

WHY IS THIS SO HARD?

can have on real estate and home ownership when the Maui wildfires swept through, devastating homes and making acres and acres of land uninhabitable.

These are just a few of the challenges that come with owning property in Hawaii, but don't worry, I'll walk you through all of this in part 3 of the book. There is a lot to learn, but when you know what to expect, you can navigate the unique challenges you'll face in this market. Throughout these pages, you'll learn exactly what to look out for and how to navigate these unique aspects of investing in paradise—especially in chapter 9. With this book, you don't have to feel like you're in the dark. Instead, you'll be prepared to invest the Pono Way.

"I don't want to be the cause of more Hawaiians leaving their homeland. How can I do this the RIGHT way?"

That is a valid question because this is a real problem. I've seen the following happen too many times here in Hawaii: Developers and foreign investors come in, flashing cash like it's nothing to get what they want without concern for our people or culture. Buyers from Japan, China, and Korea will snatch up properties and build massive houses, but here's the kicker—they don't even live in them! They leave them sitting vacant most of the year. Meanwhile, the locals—our families, people who've been here for generations—are the ones paying the price. Let me explain.

When investors buy properties and then leave the mansions they've built empty, it drives up property taxes in the surrounding areas. Suddenly, aunties and uncles who've lived in the same homes for decades are struggling just to keep up with the taxes. It breaks my heart, because it's like they're getting priced out of their own homes, their own paradise.

That's not how I do business. My values are simple—I believe in investing in a way that supports the local community, not in a way that pushes people out. It's not just about making a profit for me. It's about making sure that our local families can stay here, that they can afford to live in the place they call home.

Hawaii doesn't need more investors who exploit people's financial situations just to make a buck. We need people who understand that real estate investing can be about so much more than just making money. It can be about helping preserve an entire culture so that future generations have something to hold onto.

This book will show you how to invest in real estate in Hawaii the Pono Way. When you lead with love and look out for the interests of others, you will naturally be contributing to Hawaiians being able to come back to the islands, owning a home they can afford, and continuing to raise the future generations of their families in Hawaii.

You're going to learn how to look for ways to build wealth while giving back to the community in ways that keep homes affordable for our people, so they don't feel forced to leave the islands. I'll show you the types of projects that bring real value, like building homes for local families or investing in properties that support long-term housing solutions.

At the end of the day, it's about respect. Respect for the land and respect for the people. I'm here to make sure our people can stay in Hawaii, not just as renters but as owners, living in the paradise we've been blessed with. That's what ethical investing means to me, and I can't wait to show you how you can get involved.

In the next chapter, I'll be revealing a secret key to investing the Pono Way that makes it possible to invest in real estate in Hawaii in a way that benefits you AND Hawaii. But first, pause a moment to take this short self-assessment to determine what might be holding you back from getting started as a real estate investor in Hawaii.

SELF-ASSESSMENT

What are your real estate investing roadblocks?

Answer the following true or false questions by circling T for True or F for False to determine the concerns that might be keeping you from taking action on your real estate investing dreams.

1. Other people's opinions have a lot of influence on me, and I often make decisions based on what will make other people happy. (T/F)

2. I feel I'm lacking the education I need to invest in real estate. (T/F)

3. I don't know how to leverage my credit or find capital. (T/F)

4. I don't know anyone who will answer the question I have about real estate investing. (T/F)

5. I'm unfamiliar with the unique challenges of the Hawaii real estate market. (T/F)

6. I don't know what I don't know when it comes to the geographic, cultural, and societal ins and outs of owning property in Hawaii. (T/F)

7. I need help knowing how to invest ethically in a way that helps keep Hawaiians from getting priced out of paradise. (T/F)

Take notice of which (if any) statements you mark with a T. These represent areas that may be holding you back from real estate investing in Hawaii. But don't worry, this book has you covered!

MAIN TAKEAWAYS FROM CHAPTER 3

1. **You don't need a degree, just a real estate investing education that you can take action on.** I didn't go to college—I went to prison. And still, I became a successful real estate investor. Why? Because I got the right education and took action. That's all it really takes. You don't need to be book smart or come from money. You just need to be willing to learn and then to do what you've learned.

2. **You can invest without using your own money.** Yes, Hawaii's real estate market is expensive, but you don't need your own money to get started. I used credit. Some of my students used home equity lines of credit. Others raised private capital. Where there's a will, there's a way. You need to stop spending money on stuff that loses value and start using it to build something that lasts.

3. **You've got to surround yourself with the right people.** When I was in prison, I had a choice—stick with the crowd that got me locked up or find people who could teach me something different. I chose something different. The same goes for you. If you want to level up, you've got to get around people who are already doing what you want to do. That's why we built the HUI Mastermind.

4. **Mainlanders can invest here—but they need to do it the right way.** Hawaii real estate is different from other markets. We've got kuleana lands, leaseholds, lava zones—you name it. If you're from the mainland and you want to invest here, that's fine. But do it the Pono Way. Respect the land. Respect the culture. Don't be part of the problem. Be part of the solution that helps keep Hawaiians in Hawaii.

Chapter 4

Building Trust with Hawaiians

D id you know that the key to everything I'm going to teach you from here on out actually has nothing to do with real estate? At least not on the surface. Without this one key element, you're really going to struggle in the Hawaii real estate market. What is it? Trust.

Real estate investing the Pono Way, using the HUI Framework, helps native Hawaiians to stop getting priced out of paradise and to start building the kind of lives they want in TWO ways.

First, it provides a side hustle or career for native Hawaiians—and mainlanders, too—who want a way to gain time and financial freedom. As long as a person has the right education and is willing to work, it can be done even if you don't have your own capital or money to invest.

Real estate investing the Pono Way also has a wider impact. When people like you ethically invest in real estate in Hawaii with the goal of looking out for others, affordable housing opportunities are created for native Hawaiians. This preserves the Hawaiian culture and way of life.

But succeeding as a real estate investor all depends on your ability to find deals. Without deals, you're stuck at the starting line with no race in sight. When you know how to find deals, determine which ones are profitable, and present the deal to someone with money who can fund it, you're ready to buy and fix or build and sell. Then repeat!

In the last chapter, I mentioned some of the unique challenges with the land from a cultural or a geographical standpoint. It pays to do your homework, and we'll talk more about how to do that and what to look out for in chapter 9. But at the very beginning, before any hands are shaken or the ink is dried, investing the Pono Way all comes down to TRUST. How do you get the developers and property owners to trust you?

There are four common questions about the tricky balancing act Hawaii real estate investors face. The answers to these questions will help you navigate building a profitable business with what's in the best interest of Hawaii's people and the land. In the rest of this chapter, I'm going to break down these questions and their answers. You'll see that trust is at the center of them all. If you follow my advice and put these answers to work, you'll be taking action while positioning yourself to profit by leading with what's best for Hawaii. And following the Pono Way is what will earn you the trust of both property owners and developers.

QUESTION #1: WHAT CAUSES THE DISTRUST HAWAIIAN PROPERTY OWNERS HAVE TOWARD REAL ESTATE INVESTORS?

Native Hawaiian or not, if you're thinking about real estate investing, you need to be aware of the general distrust many Hawaiians have of outside real estate investors. Where does it come from? It all started in 1898, when the United States annexed the Hawaiian Islands. Around 1.8 million acres of land that used to belong to the Kingdom of Hawaii was taken from native Hawaiians without compensation.

You can see how that would cause some trust issues, right? As a collective people, we've learned the hard way that money in the right hands can do good, but money in the wrong hands can do damage. Unfortunately, many real estate investors haven't done much to help undo the damage that was caused by the US government annexing so much land.

Part of being a real estate investor is identifying and analyzing deals. Information is powerful, and you have to do your research. Unfortunately, many real estate investors use information solely for their own benefits. They watch properties and look specifically for situations where people can't afford to pay their mortgages. They wait until the property is almost in foreclosure before swooping in and offering to "help" homeowners, convincing them to sign over their property and leaving them with nothing.

I mentioned before that one of my first deals was with an older woman in poor health who couldn't afford her mortgage payments anymore. She had no family and no way to care for the property, which was far too big for her to maintain. I partnered up with another investor, and we took over her mortgage payments. But instead of leaving her with nothing, we tapped into our coaches' expertise to provide her with cash up front and at the end of the deal. We also found her a nice apartment and got her a car. In the end, we made profit, and she benefited, too. But it doesn't always work like that, and sometimes I think about how differently that could have turned out had she been approached first by an investor only out for money.

Ask any Hawaiian and they'll either have a story like this or know someone who's had a negative past experience with a high maka maka investor who came in, bought up land, tore down affordable housing, and built mansions that nobody even lives in. The native Hawaiians are the ones left to deal daily with rising real estate prices and increasing property taxes. And that leaves a bad taste in people's mouths.

QUESTION #2: HOW DO I GET HAWAIIAN PROPERTY OWNERS TO TRUST ME?

The great thing about Hawaii is there are deals everywhere. How you approach finding deals plays a big part in building trust and making a positive impression on the people you'll be doing deals *with*. To build trust, you have to put your boots on the ground and build strong, healthy relationships.

Let's say you decide to hop in the car and drive around. I call these "Drive for Dollars" because you'll definitely see potential deals. But look closer. Behind every run-down or empty, beat-up house you see, there's a person with a story. What if you first reached out personally and just listened to their story before you approached them as a real estate investor?

Going directly to the owner might be slower than working with a realtor or cold calling homeowners, but I believe in keeping things personal—putting in the work myself, right here in the community. That's how I built my reputation. I am known as someone who respects the land and the people. I'm not just looking to make a quick buck, and I really want to help local families hold onto a piece of home.

I show up to talk in person. I share my story with them so they know I'm one of them, not just another developer without a heart. I get to know their families and look out for their wishes and needs. It makes a big difference!

Now, what if you're a mainland investor who can't show up for face-to-face conversations? One way to overcome this hurdle is to have a connection in Hawaii who can do it for you. I know real estate investors who've used a friend or family member who lives in the islands. You could also connect with a local realtor on the phone or via email.

In part two of this book, I will show you some more ways to look for deals. This is information that normally only my HUI Mastermind students have access to, but because you're reading this book, you're family now, and family looks out for each other.

QUESTION #3: HOW DO I COME ACROSS AS TRUSTWORTHY IN MY MARKETING?

You want people to know you're looking for deals, but you don't have to get fancy about it. In fact, when you're first getting started, the more you try to play the part of the slick real estate investor with a shiny car and fancy suit who swoops in and out, the more people will hold you at arm's length. In the early days, I used to put up temporary bandit signs—those temporary plant-it-in-the-dirt-and-go roadside signs—and take out ads on Craigslist that said, "Fuzzy Buys Houses in Cash" and my number. I went straight to the point, local style.

This simple message was effective at reaching property owners who needed a quick, hassle-free sale. It wasn't long before developers and folks with properties they were thinking about selling started to reach out directly to me. Those ads connected me to some great deals, stuff that wasn't even listed. Because of this, I wasn't competing with a bunch of other buyers, and that made a huge difference. It's like finding a secret spot only you know about and being able to catch more fish because no one else is fishing there.

QUESTION #4: WHO SHOULD I CONNECT WITH TO HELP ME BUILD TRUST WITH LOCALS?

You know how they say, "It's not just WHAT you know, it's WHO you know"? That's 100% true when it comes to gaining the trust of Hawaiian property owners. When you make connections with trustworthy people, you're seen as trustworthy, and you can then leverage those connections to make even more connections.

Get to know your local real estate agents—the good ones that locals like and use. Talk to other investors who have been doing deals locally for a while. Find out who the listing agents are and make friends with them. Each of these people can become someone who can help you make connections that build trust with Hawaiian property owners.

For those of you investing from the mainland, work with local developers and get involved in community-based projects. This shows locals that you're invested in what matters to them, not just what will profit you. Hawaii is a place of incredible beauty and history, and your approach to investing here should reflect an understanding of both of those areas. This isn't just about owning land. It's about becoming part of a larger story and ensuring that future generations of native Hawaiians will still have a place to call home.

QUESTION #5: HOW SHOULD I APPROACH DEALS?

Approach deals the Pono Way by looking for those that will have a good outcome for everyone. Of course you want to make a profit, but you can still do that while keeping the needs of native Hawaiians in mind. That way everyone wins. So what do deals like this look like?

Look for opportunities that support both local communities and financial growth. For me, the ideal properties are those that make it possible to give back to the land and the people. I'm talking about places that aren't just faceless assets. They're pieces of paradise that Hawaiians can own, pass down, or use to build wealth without losing their cultural roots. This means looking for properties that allow for sustainable use and long-term value, not just quick returns or high-turnover rentals, which can be a lot of work on the property management side.

Properties with potential for multigenerational ownership or co-ops can be great assets, especially in communities where high costs tend to push families out. Co-op housing—where multiple families live together in one home—or even fixer-uppers in up-and-coming areas allow family members to work together, invest, and expand gradually. These setups create opportunities for families to stay rooted in Hawaii and help each other succeed, rather than being at the mercy of outside buyers.

BEYOND TRUST

Building trust is the key to landing your first real estate deal and every deal after that. It may take a bit longer to put in the time to build relationships and do your research on the right types of opportunities, but it's worth it when you realize you're helping others.

Remember that first deal I worked on with an elderly woman on the Big Island who was really struggling? She was living alone in a home that had become too large and too expensive to manage. Her mortgage payments were becoming unmanageable, and she was on the verge of losing the home. With the help of my coaches and another student, we stepped in to take over her payments...but we didn't stop there.

We also found her a smaller, more affordable rental where she felt safe and comfortable. We even bought her a car to help her regain a bit of independence and mobility. It wasn't just about the property. It was about helping her get back on her feet and making sure she had what she needed to feel secure again.

Real estate investing should be about more than the transaction. For me, this deal reinforced that real estate investing the Pono Way can have an amazing, positive impact on a person. Being able to help someone else reminded me that real estate wasn't just about buildings—it's about people and their stories.

MAIN TAKEAWAYS FROM CHAPTER 4

1. **Trust is the foundation of everything in Hawaiian real estate.** If you're going to invest in real estate in Hawaii, you need to understand one thing—none of it works without trust. Because of our history of being burned before, Hawaiians don't trust just anyone, especially when it comes to land. If you want to do business here, you've got to earn that trust through your actions, not just your words.

2. **Your reputation is your currency in this market.** Deals come from the relationships you create. I built my business by showing up in the community, helping people, and treating every deal like it involved my own family. That's how people came to know me, trust me, and want to work with me.

3. **Investing the Pono Way means doing what's right, even when no one's looking.** This isn't about squeezing every dollar out of a deal. It's about helping people stay in their homes, creating win-win situations, and protecting the culture and community we love. That's what it means to invest with heart. That's what it means to invest the Pono Way.

4. **Real estate is about more than buildings—it's about people.** Behind every property is a person, a story, and a situation. If you lead with Aloha and listen before you act, you'll not only make better deals—you'll make a real difference. That's what separates a real estate investor from a community builder.

Chapter 5

The Catch

If trust is the key to real estate investing, why isn't everyone who wants to get into it an instant success? If all you have to do is build trust, shouldn't becoming a profitable real estate investor be easy?

I never promised it would be easy, remember? While real estate investing is pretty simple, it still takes work. Even if you were the most trustworthy, well-connected person on the island, having those qualities still wouldn't be enough to guarantee you'd be successful. You still need to learn the HOW of investing in Hawaii real estate.

For that, you need the HUI Framework.

THE OTHER GUYS

Of course, the HUI Framework isn't your only option when it comes to learning the how-to of real estate investing. There are plenty of other real estate investing coaches who have courses or programs. But look out for the ones who are really only interested in selling their programs. To them, selling is a numbers game. They're good at it, and they care more about their bottom lines than they do about their students.

They drop big bucks on commercials and ads with good hooks. They know how to grab people's attention by talking about the problems they're experiencing and their dreams for a better life. Then they position becoming a real estate investor as the solution to the problems that people face. They're slick marketers, and they know how to tug on people's feelings.

How do I know? Because I've been targeted by them all before. They get you to sign up for a seminar, then once they've got you in the room, they lay it all out there like this:

"...so, if you're ready to change your life with real estate investing, we'd love for you to join our team!"

It sounds like a dream come true...until they announce it's $50,000 to become a team member. That's out of reach for most people. The education may be good, but it's financially unattainable for most native Hawaiians. And most of the time, there's nothing specific to Hawaii real estate in their education—that's a real problem, because real estate investing in Hawaii is unlike investing in real estate anywhere else in the world.

WHAT YOU REALLY NEED

Earning trust is vital for success. However, practical "how-to" education about investing in Hawaii real estate is also necessary. Additionally, you'll need to learn how to leverage the trust to find, analyze, and fund deals.

You need information on the history and pitfalls specific to the Hawaii real estate market so you don't make missteps that hold you back or harm the people or the land. There are different rules and regulations, different cultural concerns—even the geography affects how real estate investing is done. What applies on the mainland doesn't always work here.

Plus, you need a framework you can follow that will take you from your first deal to building a team and scaling your real estate investing business.

I've been where you are. In a way, I AM you. What better place to learn from than someone like you? I've been investing in real estate in Hawaii for more than 10 years. My main goal isn't to sell you something. I just want to help by giving you the real estate investing education you need to pull yourself up out of the bucket and achieve time and financial freedom the Pono Way.

And that's something the $50,000 gurus don't do.

I'm so glad you're reading this book right now. In the next few chapters, I'm going to teach you the entire HUI Framework. We'll take a deep dive into the Hawaii real estate market. You'll learn how to invest in real estate the Pono Way, with a heart full of Aloha and trust. And you'll learn how to get started using other people's money.

MAIN TAKEAWAYS FROM CHAPTER 5

1. **It's simple, but it's not easy.** I'll be real with you—real estate investing isn't a get-rich-quick scheme or some kind of magic. It takes real time, real effort, and a lot of ongoing learning. Yet, once you understand the fundamentals and consistently apply them, the core process is quite simple. That's why I teach the HUI Framework—to make real estate investing in Hawaii clear, doable, and repeatable for anyone willing to put in the work.

2. **Not all coaching is created equal.** There are a lot of slick marketers out there who'll charge you $50,000 for a real estate course that barely scratches the surface and doesn't teach anything about investing in Hawaii specifically. That's not me. I created the HUI Framework to give locals a real shot. No hype. Just heart, strategy, and results.

3. **You need a framework that's built for Hawaii.** This isn't the mainland. Hawaii has different rules, a different culture, and different land issues. If you try to use a one-size-fits-all real estate system here, you're gonna run into problems. The HUI Framework will help you navigate this market the right way.

4. **You already have what it takes—you just need to start.** You're not missing anything. You don't need to be smarter, richer, or luckier. You need a plan, a little guidance, and the guts to take action. That's what this book is about. You've already got the heart—now, let's get to work.

PART 2

The HUI Framework

Chapter 6

What is the Pono Way?

The most important thing to build your real estate investing business has less to do with the WHAT of real estate investing, and more to do with the heart behind it— your WHY. If you want to invest in Hawaii real estate in a way that benefits everyone involved, you must approach everything you do in the Pono Way. I've mentioned the Pono Way several times already in this book, and before I dive into the HUI Framework, it's important to get clear on what the Pono Way is when it comes to real estate investing and how it fits into the HUI Framework picture.

When you invest in real estate in Hawaii the Pono Way, you honor and respect the land, the people, and the culture of the islands while still creating opportunities for financial growth. This is personal for me, and it should be personal for you, too.

Real success is about giving back to the community and ensuring locals have a path to wealth that doesn't force them out of their homelands. Hawaii is more than just a beautiful place. It's my home and a place rich with history, tradition, and family values. Investing the Pono Way means embracing these values and prioritizing them over pure profit.

At the heart of the Pono Way is the principle of *stewardship*. We believe land ownership isn't about control but is actually about responsibility. This land has stories, and these stories connect us to our ancestors. When I invest, it's not just a transaction. It's about understanding the true value of each piece of land physically and culturally and finding ways to use that value to benefit the local community, not just the investor. That's why I focus on projects that create housing options for locals and support the preservation of our unique Hawaiian way of life.

Community support and empowerment are also key aspects of the Pono Way. Hawaii's real estate market is challenging for sure. Prices are high, and many locals feel they can't afford to stay. I want to show people they can create wealth and security here without having to give up their culture or community. Through education and mentorship, I help Hawaiians learn how to build financial independence, using real estate as a tool to stay in their homeland and protect it.

LEARNING THE PONO WAY

It still blows my mind how much a little knowledge can change someone's entire financial future. For example, my uncle was like a lot of locals here in Hawaii—hardworking, blue-collar, and trusting the system he was taught to believe in. He had a regular 401(k), the kind that rides the stock market roller coaster, and he was watching it tank after the market crashed.

One day, I told him, "Uncle, you don't have to sit there watching your retirement disappear. You can take control of it. Ever heard of a self-directed IRA?" I could tell he didn't really believe me, so I explained it the way I wish someone had explained it to me years earlier.

"Look," I said, "your 401(k) is tied up in whatever Wall Street decides to do, right? But if you roll the money into a self-directed IRA, you can invest it in real estate." Up to that point, he'd never thought about real estate investing a day in his life, so I walked him through the process, step-by-step. We got on the phone with a company that sets up self-directed IRAs and opened an account. Then I showed him how to use the account to invest in real estate deals.

The first deal we did together was a small fixer-upper here on the island. We pooled his retirement funds and some money I'd raised from other investors to buy it, fix it up, and flip it. When that first check hit his account, I'll never forget the look of surprise and pride on his face.

"This ain't like the stock market," he said. "I can actually see it. Touch it. We made this happen."

That moment was bigger than just closing a deal. It was about breaking the cycle of dependency on a system that wasn't built for people like us. My uncle didn't just grow his retirement with that deal. He grew his confidence. He saw he could take control and invest in something real, building a future on his own terms.

That's what drives me to keep teaching others. If my uncle, someone who was a total beginner, could do it, then you can do it, too. Sometimes, all it takes is someone showing you the way, just like I showed him.

GIVING BACK THE PONO WAY

Another fundamental value in the Pono Way is the concept of "giving back." My success is not only for me. It's for my family, my neighbors, and the generations who come after us. That's why I don't just teach the "how-to" of real estate investing. I teach ethical investing principles to encourage people to lift up others as they succeed. I want locals and outsiders to invest here on the Islands in ways that contribute to our Hawaiian community, rather than driving us out.

The Pono Way is the key to ethical real estate investing in Hawaii because it respects the land and the people. It's about striking a balance—pursuing financial success without sacrificing the cultural and environmental integrity of Hawaii. By investing this way, we can preserve what makes Hawaii unique, support local families, and create a legacy to honor our history and sustain our future.

HOW TO APPLY THE PONO WAY TO REAL ESTATE INVESTING

What does the Pono Way look like in practical terms when it comes to real estate investing? Leading with love sounds great, but the Pono Way of real estate investing is more than an ideal. It's love in action. Let's talk about five practical ways to put the Pono Way to work inside your real estate investing business to benefit Hawaii and its people and culture. They all start with the letter P, so they'll be super easy to remember. They are: projects, people, purpose, planning, and progress.

Choosing *Projects* the Pono Way

First of all, I want you to think about what kind of properties you're buying. Could those properties be used as affordable housing options for Hawaiian natives? Yes, tourism is a huge industry here. But it doesn't benefit Hawaiians much when investors buy five luxury properties that become short-term rentals only the wealthy can afford, leaving these properties to sit empty a majority of the time. Instead, what if you turned large properties into multifamily dwellings or co-op housing options and allowed them to be rented out affordably during the off season?

Many families in Hawaii do co-op housing, where multiple families live together and pool their resources so they can save money to buy more properties over time. This is a great strategy that works, especially considering the high cost of living in Hawaii, which is why this solution appeals to so many families.

They start small by buying an affordable condo or apartment. Then they live below their means for a while, fix up the place, and sell it or rent it out. This allows them to build up capital for future real estate investments, and it can be a great way for you to get started, too.

When it comes to new building projects, consider foregoing the expensive builds and go with reasonably priced houses and multifamily units affordable for Hawaiians looking to buy or rent. Expensive builds are outside the purchasing budget for most Hawaiians and often sit empty part of the year. By providing affordable housing options, you're helping preserve the culture that makes Hawaii such a wonderful place to live and visit. You can be a part of helping Hawaiians rise collectively by making it possible for them to leverage community and family support as a means to overcome economic challenges and to build wealth in Hawaii's expensive real estate market. The Pono Way means you become part of the solution.

Hiring *People* the Pono Way

Next, consider who you hire. If you have a building project or need people to do the property maintenance and management, why not hire locals? Hire Hawaiian-owned construction companies, electricians, plumbers, and landscapers. This puts money back into the local economy and directly impacts the bank accounts of local families.

Ask around to learn who comes highly recommended and check out their reviews on their websites and Google Business. It is helpful to look for locals who have a similar mindset as you about stewardship and responsibility.

Setting Your *Purpose* the Pono Way

When I first started thinking about real estate investing, I was overwhelmed. I remember asking myself, "How the heck am I going to do this?" Living in Hawaii, the numbers were intimidating—it was going to take half a million dollars or more just to get started. I felt like that was almost impossible. Where was I going to come up with that kind of money?

My business partner in HUI Mastermind, Zasha Smith, struggled with her mindset, too. She grew up thinking she'd work a steady job until retirement at 67, then enjoy life. That's what everybody else did, so what other option was there? When she bought her first home, a fixer-upper, she remembers wondering, "How the heck are all these people buying rental properties? They must have a lot of money or come from money!" But the more she looked into real estate investing, the more her mindset changed.

Zasha saw retirees coming to Hawaii for the first time ever, and she realized she didn't want to wait until retirement to really start living. She wanted to find a way to generate income that didn't take up all her time so she could enjoy Hawaii now AND later. That became her purpose and her deep "why."

I could totally relate. I had watched my parents work hard their whole lives. We didn't spend much quality time together growing up because they were always working. I didn't want to spend my life grinding just to barely make it. I wanted more for my family and more for myself. Yes, I wanted the freedom to surf when I wanted and to travel to Disney World and Disneyland to make memories with my wife and daughter.

But deeper than that, it was heartbreaking to watch more and more native Hawaiians leave the Islands because of how expensive it is to live here. I wanted to have an impact and help make it more affordable for natives to stay. That's my "why" and my deep purpose.

Before we ever met each other, Zasha and I both came to the conclusion that real estate investing was the solution. We invested in the education we needed to put our dreams to work. We both focused on our deep "why"—the thing that made us committed to real estate investing, even when it got hard.

Everything has its own set of challenges, and if you think new adventures are going to be smooth sailing all the time, you're mistaken. Without a sense of purpose behind what you do, you won't stick with something when the going gets tough. Refusing to give up on doing what's right—that's the Pono Way. Having a deep "why" makes all the difference because it will keep you in the game when the challenges come.

My "why" pushed me to get educated, to take risks, and to step outside my comfort zone. It gave me the courage to learn about leveraging property-related equity, exploring different financing options, and partnering with others to achieve my goals. Above all, my "why" helped me stick with real estate investing even when my mindset needed work.

Your mindset will need work, too, when you get started real estate investing. Don't be surprised when you feel like you're having to rearrange your brain to make room for new realizations and discoveries about who you are and what you're capable of. For me, one big mindset breakthrough came on a coaching call. I'd paid $26,000 to join a real estate investment coaching program. That was a lot of money for me, and I was nervous. Where was I going to find the money to invest in real estate when $26,000 for real estate investing education seemed like a lot?

Then one of my coaches said something I'll never forget, and it hit me hard. "Throw out what you think you know. Forget about the money you don't have. If you can find a good deal, the money will come." That conversation blew my mind. I realized my limiting beliefs were holding me back. It wasn't about having the money upfront. It was about seeing opportunities and connecting the dots.

Once I realized this, I was able to recognize opportunities and see this concept work firsthand. For example, one of my first deals was found by another coaching program student. The coach funded the project, and I helped make things happen by fixing up the property to sell. When the property sold, I had made back almost half the money I'd invested in the coaching program without using a dime of my own money on the project—in just ONE deal. That moment was life-changing because it taught me that my mindset, not my bank account, had been my biggest obstacle to success.

The next deal I did was one for the record books. I took the profits from my first deal plus money from other project partners who invested with me, and I paid $165,000 for a property. The house was in a challenging spot. Not only was it in a lava flow area, but it was in an area that had recently experienced a hurricane.

We didn't back down, though. We stuck it out and made it through every setback. After months of hard work, we finally sold that house for $265,000. Seeing that number felt like hitting the jackpot—not just because of the cash, but because of what it meant. We'd faced down nature itself and still came out on top. I'll talk more about lava flows and how they can affect how you choose projects in chapter 9.

I walked away with a 12% return. It wasn't the biggest piece of the pie, but it was enough to keep me fired up. My partners, who put in more capital, earned even bigger returns, which was exactly how we structured the deal. We all won because we kept going no matter what. Deals like that remind me why I do this—why I keep showing up, keep investing, and keep believing in what's possible—no matter what comes my way.

Looking back, I can see that tapping into my purpose and discovering my deep "why" created the biggest mindset shifts for me, and your purpose can do the same for you. Your "why" has to be so strong and clear that nothing can stop you. Remember, it's not just about making money. It's about what that money allows you to do. For me, it's about providing for my family, building affordable housing for others, and giving back to my community. That's my compass, and it keeps me moving toward my true north, no matter what challenges come my way.

Planning the Pono Way

The next step to investing in real estate the Pono Way is planning. It starts with setting goals, which are so important because unless you have something planned out, you can't achieve it. Getting clear and specific about your goals will give you the ability to create a step-by-step action plan to achieve your objectives.

Goal setting and planning have always been important to me. I've been a waterman my whole life. I know the ocean better than anything else. When I was younger, I was a professional surfer. Even back then, I set goals to become one of the best in my field, and I was specific about what that looked like for me. I wanted to be in the magazines as one of the top athletes in that industry. I knew that to be the best, I needed to set milestones and attainable goals. It's okay to shoot for the stars, but it's important to start out by setting goals that are realistic and reachable. Then, you can aim higher.

There are many ways to set and track goals. To make it easy, I've created a downloadable *Getting Started Guide*, and I will tell you how to access it and walk you through it in chapter 10 of this book.

As you set goals, it really helps to break them into daily, weekly, monthly, and quarterly steps. It can be intimidating staring at a big goal, but when you break it down so that you can take one step at a time and chart your path to completion, it will feel much more manageable. Breaking things down step by step is also a great way to hold yourself accountable in a way that lets you see the action you're taking and the progress you're making. You can share your goals with someone else for accountability, too.

Once you have things laid out step-by-step, clear some time in your calendar to get to work on those goals. I take action on my goals by keeping a weekly schedule prioritizing my activities and tasks according to their importance in my life. Family time is the most important to me, so every day I wake up, take my daughter to school, and make sure she's all set for the day.

After dropping off my daughter, I manage all the projects I have going on. I spend time talking with contractors and subcontractors and staying on top of accounts. My daughter plays golf, so after school I pick her up and drive her to practice. As a family, we travel together for her tournaments. Running my own business as a real estate investor allows me to be there at every tournament, no matter how far it is from home. I wouldn't have it any other way.

But what do you do if you aren't sure which smaller steps will lead you to your bigger goals? I've got that covered in the next section.

REVERSE ENGINEERING YOUR GOALS

Need an example of how to set an achievable goal? I like to do what I call the reverse engineer method for goal setting. Here's how it works:

Let's say one of your goals is to get your first fix-and-flip this year. Your first step is to figure out what you need to do each quarter to get closer to that goal. Maybe you need to put in 100 offers or find 1,000 off-market deals. Maybe you need to contact 20 realtors every month. That's a lot to bite off all at once, isn't it?

Instead, make it manageable. Break it down into actionable daily, weekly, and monthly steps that make it easy to get started. A daily step for this goal might be to make ten calls every day to realtors or other lead sources like wholesalers. A weekly goal might be to Drive for Dollars—take a drive through neighborhoods looking for potential deals, and make connections with property owners. A monthly goal might be to follow up and follow back with people who have responded to your calls and connection attempts. Write down each step, giving it a trackable number of connections or contacts, then record your progress as you go.

Making *Progress* the Pono Way

Part of investing in real estate, the Pono Way, is staying at the top of your game and continuing to grow as a person. I want to share something that has made a huge difference in my life when it comes to the progress I make in my business—reading mindset and professional development books. There will be times in business and life when you'll need a little extra help and support. In those instances, it's a great idea to have some good resources on hand. If you really want to level up your mindset, here are my top recommendations—these books have changed my life by transforming my mindset.

I recommend these books to all my HUI Mastermind members, and I highly suggest you add them to your collection now, so that you can start benefiting from their wisdom right away.

> *Rich Dad Poor Dad* by Robert Kiyosaki helped me shift my mindset about money and investing. It taught me to think beyond the traditional "work until retirement" approach.

> *The Miracle Morning* by Hal Elrod helped me establish a morning routine and stay consistent in my efforts to grow my real estate business.

> *Atomic Habits* by James Clear has great strategies for building consistent habits. Taking consistent action

and developing good habits are essential for the success of your real estate business.

The E-Myth Revisited by Michael E. Gerber taught me how to be a business owner and not a technician inside my business, which saves me tons of time and energy.

The E-Myth Real Estate Investor by Michael E. Gerber, Than Merrill, and Paul Esajian present the E-Myth strategy specific to real estate investors. It's a great book too!

How to Win Friends and Influence People by Dale Carnegie taught me how to network and build relationships, which is super important for a real estate investor. I'm always dealing with contractors, real estate agents, and homeowners.

Awaken the Giant Within by Tony Robbins and *Napoleon Hill's Keys to Success* by Napoleon Hill were also life-changing books for me. I read both of those while I was in prison, and I include information from both inside HUI Mastermind.

Reading these books will help you learn how to develop good business building habits and mindsets, two important skills to develop as you get started.

By now, you can see why I believe so deeply in doing real estate the Pono Way. This isn't just about flipping properties or chasing big checks. This is a way to do right by our people, our land, and our future. The truth is, Hawaii needs more investors with heart, and if you've read this far, I know you've got what it takes. But belief alone won't move the needle—you need a plan, and that's exactly what you're about to get.

In the next part of this book, I'm going to walk you through the step-by-step process I've used to build my business from the ground up using the HUI Framework. This is where things get real. You'll learn how to structure your business, find and analyze deals, make offers, and fund your projects—all without using your own money or time. So let's get to it.

MAIN TAKEAWAYS FROM CHAPTER 6

1. **The Pono Way means leading with heart, respect, and responsibility.** Pono is more than just a word—it's a way of life. It means doing what's right, even when nobody's watching. It means honoring the land, respecting the people, and making choices that keep the Aloha alive for future generations. When you carry yourself the Pono Way, you bring integrity into everything you do—including your business.

2. **You apply the Pono Way to real estate by putting people before profit.** In this game, it's easy to get caught up chasing numbers. But the Pono Way flips that. It's about creating deals that work for everyone. That means helping families stay in their homes, making deals that keep housing affordable, and finding solutions that serve the community—not just your wallet.

3. **Planning your real estate business the Pono Way starts with clarity.** Before you build anything, you need to get clear on your "why." What are you building this for? Who are you doing this for? When you've got that locked in, you can make smart decisions driven by your values and that align with the kind of legacy you want to leave behind.

4. **You have to reverse engineer your goals to get where you want to go.** Don't just dream big—break those dreams down in a way that allows you to take action. Start with the end result you want, then work backward to figure out the steps it takes to get there. That's how I built my business, and that's how I teach my HUI students to move forward, too. When you know your destination, the path becomes a lot clearer.

Chapter 7.0

Introduction to the HUI Framework

Welcome to the HUI Framework, my step-by-step process for investing in Hawaiian estate the Pono Way. There are nine main steps in the HUI Framework that I'll work through in this chapter. I've divided each stage into its own section.

Read the chapters in order, making notes as you go. Here's a quick preview of what's covered in chapter 7, section by section:

Chapter 7.1: Setting Up Your Business
Chapter 7.2: The Buying Process
Chapter 7.3: Building a Dream Team
Chapter 7.4: Finding Deals
Chapter 7.5: Analyzing Deals
Chapter 7.6: Making Offers
Chapter 7.7: Funding Deals
Chapter 7.8: Closing the Deal
Chapter 7.9: Managing the Project

Once you've read through chapter 7, you'll have my entire HUI Framework—the same one I teach the students inside my HUI Academy and Mastermind. I want you to have a really good jumpstart to your real estate investing business so in part 3 of this book, I'll go even deeper into the blessings and challenges specific to the Hawaii real estate market. Then in part 4, you'll have the chance to take action by setting goals, getting your financial benchmarks arranged, and building your own real estate investing business plan.

Chapter 7.1

Setting Up Your Business

The first stage of the HUI Framework is setting up your business, which is one of the first things people interested in real estate investing ask me about. They want to know if they should write a formal business plan, create an LLC, or hire a bunch of professionals like accountants and lawyers. They're always a little surprised by my initial answer.

The truth is until you land your first deals, you can do almost everything under your own name. There's no one right way. You have to consider what fits your current budget and legal needs and go from there. I'm going to walk you step-by-step through what you will need, but before we get too far into this chapter on business set up, I want to give a disclaimer.

This book is a story of inspiration that gives strategies and tactics that have worked for me as I grew my real estate investing business. If I can do it, you can do it, too. However, I am not a lawyer or financial expert. The best way to protect yourself is to talk to an attorney or legal consultation company so they can point you in the right direction. For legal or financial advice, contact a professional.

When I first started in real estate investing, I didn't rush to set up a business. My early projects were done through my coaches' companies. They had all the legal and financial stuff covered, so I didn't need my own LLC right away. As I grew my business, I knew it was time to get serious about creating my own company and everything that went along with that in order to protect myself and my assets. I formed an LLC, created social media profiles, designed a logo, and printed some business cards. I even used Fiverr.com for branding materials because it was affordable and effective.

FORMING AN LLC

When it comes to getting started, one of the first things to consider is how to protect your personal assets. At first, you can start your business under your personal name. That's what many new investors do, especially if you're applying for conventional loans, which typically require a personal name. But beware—it's the unforeseen issues that will get you if you're not prepared. Protecting yourself legally is important, and you will eventually want to set up your business under an LLC. Without an LLC, you're not protected from lawsuits or liability if there happens to be an accident at a project site.

At one of my projects, a builder fell off a roof at a work site. Thank goodness he wasn't hurt, but if he had been, his family could have sued. If I didn't have an LLC, I personally could have been held liable. Consult an attorney or legal service to set up your business the right way.

You can create the paperwork on LegalZoom for free and then pay the filing and registration fees, or you can use a paid service, tax professional, or lawyer to create the forms and file them for you. Fees vary state to state, so check your state's website. To file the Articles of Organization for an LLC in Hawaii, it costs $50. You'll also be required to file an annual report each year for $15.[1] Other fees apply for amendments and additional changes.

I used Nevada Corporate Headquarters to create my LLC. Their agents can help you manage your portfolio, take care of the paperwork and filings, help create business plans, and help with your taxes. Prime Corporate Services is another great option. Zasha used it to set up her LLC, and they offer free consulting. For more information about Prime Corporate Services, see the Resources section of this book. You can also set it up yourself by contacting your state's business office, but make sure to track your accounting from day one.

No matter who you use to help form your LLC, make sure to include an operating agreement. This structure will protect you as you add team members (I will share more about adding team members in section 7.3) and will keep things organized so everyone knows what their roles are. Even if you're a solo investor, you can outline future roles and property management plans.

HAVING PROFESSIONAL EXPERTS IN YOUR POCKET

Once you form an LLC, you want to start thinking about connecting with some professional insurance, law, and financial experts. First, consider hiring a certified public accountant or tax professional. Having these skilled professionals on your team will save you headaches as your business grows. I also recommend a bookkeeper to keep your numbers tidy and keep your accountant happy.

Next, if you're going to do building or fix-and-flip projects, make sure you have good insurance. For that, you'll need blanket coverage for the projects to ensure all the contractors for your projects are covered. I use Pyramid Insurance, an insurance broker, to help me find good builder's risk insurance.

Finally, a good real estate lawyer is key to helping you draft contracts and other legal documents. Could you use LegalZoom? Yes, but as you become more established, you'll want to have a lawyer you can trust to read through all your documents and agreements. There are many in real estate—purchase contract agreements, assignment fee agreements, and trust agreements, to name a few. Although these documents are pretty straightforward, a lawyer will help ensure all the i's are dotted and t's are crossed. Make sure the lawyers you work with are familiar with the laws and regulations in the areas you want to invest in. A good lawyer or escrow company is also helpful when you need to do deed transfers and quick liens. You don't have to have a lawyer or escrow company on retainer. Just have a few good ones in your contacts when you need legal documents created or reviewed.

So where and how do you find these professionals? Word of mouth is my favorite way to connect with experts. Ask people you trust, like your family and friends. They're not going to steer you wrong. If all else fails, check local listings, walk through the Yellow Pages, and read Google or Better Business Bureau reviews.

CREATING AN ONLINE PRESENCE

After creating an LLC, you'll want to turn your attention to promoting your business and get the word out about your desire to invest in real estate. For that, you'll need an online presence. If people can't find you online, it will be difficult for them to approach you with opportunities. There are a couple ways you can create an online presence: build a website, create social media profiles, or do both and link them all together.

If you have more time than money, start by creating social media profiles on all major platforms like Facebook, Instagram, LinkedIn, X (formerly known as Twitter), YouTube, and TikTok. Social media profiles and pages are free to create, and you can use social media content to grab people's attention and get the word out that you're looking for deals. As you create your profiles, try to use the same handle for all of them. For example, you can find me on all the major platforms as @hifuzz.

Does social media content help you get deals? Absolutely! Social media has helped me land so many clients and projects. Posting consistently on my social media platforms helped people get to know, like, and trust me. Then, when an opportunity for us to work together presented itself, they were in! When interest rates went up a few years ago, the banks here had a deal for 5% interest on Certificate of Deposit accounts (also called CDs). My investors make 10–12% back on their investments, so I did one live video about why real estate is a better investment than putting your money in a bank account.

Because of that one video, someone sent me a direct message asking if I needed any money to fund future projects. I met with this person at his home and explained how everything works. I drafted a contract, and he deposited the funds I needed for the build—$200,000. My team built the home, and the house is in escrow right now. He'll make 10%–12% from his investment, instead of 5% from the banks. This deal is a win-win for everyone.

Even though you may not need one right away, eventually, you will want a website. I like Carrot.com for real estate websites because they simplify SEO, or search engine optimization, so buyers and sellers can find you easily. If you want something simpler, try Wix.com or Square.com. Both have low-cost options that allow you to build a website with easy-to-use, drag-and-drop editors. If cost isn't an issue, you can hire a website developer to build a site for you. In the beginning though, simple is best. Make sure you include:

- Who you are
- Who you help
- What you do

- What types of properties you're looking for
- How people can contact you

BUILDING YOUR BUSINESS CREDIT

Want a ninja tip as you're getting started? Establish credit for your business. Even if you don't need it right now, when the deals come, you will. Early on, I connected with LenCred, which helped me secure lines of credit and credit cards for my projects. Then I asked around to find contractors who took credit card payments, which would allow me to pay for labor and materials on credit. This strategy helped me scale fast without using my own money and allowed me to pay back while making a profit when the projects were complete.

To use business credit effectively, open a dedicated business bank account. This keeps personal liability low and makes tax time easier. You can also work with companies like Prime Corporate Services to build your business credit profile with Dun & Bradstreet (D&B), a company that keeps track of how businesses handle their money. Think of it like a credit report—but for your business, instead of you personally. When you start a legit business, you can apply for a DUNS number, which is a unique ID number that D&B gives you. It's kind of like a Social Security number but for your business. This will make securing loans and credit lines for future projects much easier. Again, this is what worked for me. Please make sure you talk to your financial advisor before making any credit decisions.

The Bottom Line

Don't overthink the business's setup when you're starting out. I've seen way too many people spend so much time worrying about setting up the business end of things that they never actually make it to the doing deals part. Focus on finding deals first. The money, partnerships, and business structure will follow. Take that first step and then build as you go.

MAIN TAKEAWAYS FROM CHAPTER 7.1

1. **Setting up your business is the first real step to protecting your business.** If you want to play the real estate game the right way, you need to act like a legitimate business owner. That means forming your LLC, getting your Employer Identification Number (EIN) which is the number used for taxes for your business, opening a business bank account, and setting up your accounting system. This isn't just red tape—it's your foundation. Once these things are in place, you're ready to start moving like a pro.

2. **Connecting with the right professionals will set you up for success.** You don't have to do this alone. Connect with a good CPA, find a business attorney you trust, and start building a relationship with a local banker. These folks will help you make smarter decisions and avoid rookie mistakes. Surround yourself with people who know what they're doing so you can focus on what you do best—find real estate deals and make them happen.

3. **Social media is your new storefront—use it wisely.** You don't need to be an influencer, but you do need to be visible. Set up a business page on Instagram and Facebook, and let people know who you are and what you do. When people see you showing up consistently, they start to see you as the go-to person for real estate. That's how you build trust and attract deals before they even hit the market.

4. **Building business credit gives you more options and more power.** Don't rely on your personal credit forever. Start establishing business credit early—get a DUNS number and keep your LLC in good standing. Over time, this opens doors to bigger funding opportunities, lower interest rates, and a whole lot more leverage that will help when it's time for your business to grow.

Chapter 7.2

The Buying Process

Before you start looking for deals, it helps to first decide how you want to approach real estate investing. There are two main decisions you need to make to influence what type of deals you go looking for: which real estate strategy you want to use and what market you want to focus on.

REAL ESTATE INVESTING STRATEGIES

Real estate investing isn't a one-size-fits-all game. It's kind of like surfing different waves. What works for one surfing spot might not work somewhere else. On top of that, here in Hawaii, we've got our own unique set of challenges and opportunities to consider. Because of the particular demands of the Hawaii real estate market, I want to share with you the four main strategies that work well in Hawaii.

Wholesaling

One of the best ways to get started in real estate investing—especially if you don't have much cash—is wholesaling. Here's how it works: You find a property, have a real estate attorney help you get it under contract, and then sell that contract to another investor for a fee. What's the beauty of this strategy? You don't need a ton of money to get started.

When I started wholesaling, I literally drove around my neighborhood to look for properties that needed help. You know the houses I'm talking about—with overgrown grass, broken-down cars in the driveway, or busted windows. Those houses scream, "Help me!" Next, I'd track down the owners and offer them a way out of their situations. Then I'd pass the deal on to an investor who had the funds to fix the properties up. (There will be more about finding investors in the Building a Dream Team section of this chapter.)

Wholesaling is one of the cheapest ways to break into real estate because all you need is hustle. Walk your neighborhood, talk to friends and family, and keep your eyes open for opportunities. Apps and programs like the resources listed in the back of this book can help, but you can also do it the old-school way—just get out there and look.

Fix-and-Flips

Another strategy that's successful in Hawaii is fixing and flipping. This is where you find a distressed property, buy it, fix it up, and sell it for a profit. You can find these deals through wholesalers, realtors, or even just driving around like you would for wholesaling.

Now, I'm not going to sugarcoat it—fixing and flipping takes more time, effort, and risk. But the rewards can be worth it. You're adding real value to the property, and when done right, you'll walk away with a nice chunk of change.

Just remember, Uncle Sam's gonna want his cut—capital gains taxes can take a bite out of your profit if you're not planning ahead. Make sure you understand how it works and talk to a tax pro. Plus, it's satisfying to see something go from rundown to remarkable. And what's even better is these properties are often affordable housing options for native Hawaiians.

New Builds

Building new homes is another strategy. This is one of my main approaches, and it's as straightforward as it sounds. You can either tear down an old house and build a new one or find a vacant lot and start from scratch. From there, you have options: flip the property for a profit, keep it as a rental, or even sell it to a family looking for their forever home.

Here in Hawaii, building new homes can be an incredible opportunity. We're always in need of affordable housing, and every project is a chance to help a local family while creating wealth for yourself at the same time. But keep in mind, this strategy requires more upfront capital and experience. It's not where most people start.

Rental Properties

During a time when the dollar doesn't stretch as far as it used to, investing your money in assets that increase in value over time—like rental properties—will yield a much better return than a savings account. If you're looking to build generational wealth, rental properties are where it's at. The idea is simple. Buy a property, rent it out, and let the tenants pay your mortgage and other expenses. Over time, you'll build equity and (hopefully) cash flow.

One of the strategies I teach for rentals in my HUI Mastermind program is called the BRRRR method: Buy, Rehab, Rent, Refinance, Repeat. You find a distressed property, fix it up, rent it out, and then refinance it to pull your money back out for the next deal. Done right, you can rinse and repeat this process over and over to build a portfolio of cash-flowing properties.

When it comes to real estate in Hawaii, you have to understand one thing right off the bat—cash flow and appreciation don't always play nice together here. Hawaii is an appreciating market, which means land and property values tend to rise over time. But finding cash flow in this environment—that's a whole different ball game. Let me break this down for you.

Cash flow comes from rental income. But in Hawaii, property prices are high and rental income rarely matches up with the costs. For example, you might buy a property, but the rent barely covers the mortgage, let alone gives you any extra money to pocket. That's why, when I'm looking for cash flow, I focus on properties where I can add value through renovations—whether it's by legally adding extra bedrooms, bathrooms, or even creating additional units and making the property suitable as a co-op housing option. This strategy helps offset costs and turns a property that's just breaking even into one that's cash-flow positive.

Hawaii's real estate market is unique because of its natural scarcity—land here is limited, and demand is always high. That's why appreciation is such a big deal. You might purchase a property today and see its value grow significantly in just a few years. Sometimes, that means paying the mortgage out of your own pocket for a while, covering costs until the rents catch up with the value. But that's the trade-off in a market like this: The long-term gain can be worth the short-term stretch.

For me, real estate in Hawaii is all about balancing cash flow with appreciation. I look for properties where I can make the numbers work—buying at a discount, adding value, and setting myself up for future gains. And let me tell you, the land itself often holds more value than the structures on it.

Commercial Properties

Last but not least, there's commercial real estate—we're talking storefronts, malls, apartment buildings, condos, storage units, and even hotels. These deals are bigger, more complex, and often require a team of experts to pull off. But the potential rewards are also big.

Commercial real estate isn't for everyone. It takes more money, more connections, and more know-how. But if you're willing to put in the work and surround yourself with the right people, it can be one of the most profitable strategies out there. While I don't do much commercial real estate investing, my business partner, Zasha, does.

Active vs. Passive Investing

One more thing to think about is whether you want to be an active or passive investor. Active investors are the ones finding deals, managing properties, and raising money. Passive investors, on the other hand, contribute capital to someone else's project and then sit back while their money works for them.

There's no right or wrong way to get started. It all depends on your goals and resources combined with how much time you want to spend. I started out as an active investor, but as my business grew, I've been able to take on more of a passive role in certain projects. Passive investing is nice since it allows me to spend more time with my wife and daughter.

PICKING A MARKET

Once you've chosen a strategy, the next step is picking a market. When it comes to picking your real estate market in Hawaii, start by keeping things simple. For me, I didn't need to look far. I just drove down the road and around my own neighborhood. I spotted a few houses clearly in need of work. They had busted out windows and overgrown yards, and they had a general sense of neglect about them.

That's when I started digging deeper into the area. I reached out to a local real estate agent to learn more about what houses in that neighborhood were selling for and what the numbers looked like. That's how I began to understand my market. I started doing calculations to see if my home area was going to be a good fit market for me. I learned how to look at the after-repair value (ARV) of properties in the area to determine which deals were good opportunities and which weren't. For example, if I purchased a home for $200,000 in Waianae and fixed it up, I could sell it for $500,000, leaving plenty of room for profit, even after renovations.

At this point, you might be wondering how to determine what a good price point is for you. How do you know what will be a good deal and what won't? First, calculate the sales price of the property you're looking at, then add how much renovations will cost—this is where having a general contractor or project manager on your Dream Team comes in super handy. That's how much you'll put into the deal. It might look something like this:

Sale Price of a Potential Investment Property: $250,000
Estimated Cost of Renovations: $60,000
Projected Investment: $310,000

That tells you what you'll put in. Now you need to determine what the ARV is for similar properties that have sold recently. There are a few ways to get this information. You can check the Multiple Listing Service (MLS) or ask a realtor you trust. Look for at least three properties that have sold within the last three to six months with similar square footage, the same number of bathrooms, and comparable lot sizes. Note how much the comparable properties sold for. Let's say the property you're looking at investing in is located in one of my favorite markets, Waianae. As I mentioned above, comparable properties in that area sell for around $500,000. That's a profit of almost $200,000 for you—this shows you that such a property would be a good investment!

Each market tells a different story when it comes to ARV. If I bought a property for $800,000 in Kailua, I could sell it for $1.2 million. On the North Shore, things are even more expensive, but the payoffs are bigger. A property you can buy for $1.1 million could sell for $3.3 million. The more information you know about your market, the better investing decisions you can make.

The Big Island is one of my favorite markets. The price points there are much more manageable compared to other islands. For example, I've built and sold brand-new homes in the $350,000 to $475,000 range, which is a far cry from the multimillion-dollar properties on Maui, Kauai, or Oahu. Starting in a more affordable market doesn't mean you're settling—it means you're being strategic. It's easier to find deals that make sense financially, especially when you're new to the game. Not only that, but those homes are much more affordable for native Hawaiians to purchase, which helps more Hawaiians stay in their homeland.

Start Close to Home
One of the easiest ways to start is by looking at markets close to where you live if you are already a Hawaii resident. Why? Because you already know the area, and familiarity is a huge advantage when you're just starting out. Plus, staying local means you have access to connections like friends, family, and professionals who can guide you. For my business partner, Zasha, starting locally meant she had a safety net. She could pivot easily, if needed, by moving into the property herself or by helping a family member who needed a place to stay. Having that kind of flexibility is invaluable when you're just getting started.

Match Your Market to Your Strategy
Your strategy will play a big part in determining the right

market for you. For example, if you're interested in short-term rentals like Airbnbs, you'll need to factor in Hawaii's regulations for short-term rentals. Some islands have more red tape than others, so you'll want to research which areas align with your goals.

On the other hand, if you're looking for long-term rental opportunities, islands like the Big Island might be a better fit because they offer more affordable entry points compared to Maui or Oahu where average home prices are often $1 million or more.

Do Your Homework

No matter where you decide to invest, doing your homework is critical. Driving around neighborhoods and spotting potential deals is just the start. You also need to understand the zoning laws, building regulations, and even the permitting status of properties, which I'll share more about in chapter 9. Trust me, you don't want to buy a property thinking it's a three-bedroom, two-bath, only to find out later it's officially recorded as a one-bedroom, one-bath. That kind of mistake can cost you time and money. It's better to say no to a deal that's not a good fit than to get stuck in a deal that ends up costing you money.

This is a lesson Zasha learned the hard way. One of the first rental projects she did had four units on the property. What she didn't know was that only one was actually permitted. The property was listed for sale as a three-bedroom, two-bathroom home. She used a private money lender to fund the deal, fixed it up, and put it on the market right away. They had buyers knocking on the door immediately. Everything looked like it was going to be smooth sailing...until the buying agent asked the listing agent, "Did you know this is a one-bedroom, one-bath home?"

The property was listed for sale as a three-bedroom, two-bathroom, but it was recorded at the local Department of Planning as a one-bedroom, one-bathroom home—meaning that's all that was allowed to be there. They ended up having to hire engineers, an architect, draftsmen, and an electrical engineer to add a septic tank and open up some walls to stay in line with what was permitted. The project ended up taking a lot longer than originally planned. Thankfully, she still ended the project and sale with a profit, but that isn't always the case.

When you start looking for deals, make sure the property owner gives you accurate information on things like square footage, decks, and extra bathrooms, then check it against the local Department of Planning's records. If you're not prepared, you could end up getting fined or having to redraw plans. You're also responsible for knowing what's legal, so you can give your contractors the right instructions for renovations and builds.

So, what are the regulations for different types of properties in Hawaii? I wish there was a simple answer, but there isn't. This is why I encourage you to familiarize yourself with state laws and county ordinances, because the regulations aren't the same across the board for all islands. You'll want to consider:

Zoning Compliance: Short-term rentals are only allowed in resort-zoned areas. If it's not located inside the right zone, you'll have to get a special permit, which can be difficult to obtain.

Permit Acquisition: Speaking of permits, make sure you have all the required permits or certificates specific to your county to avoid substantial fines.

Stay Informed: Regulations change over time. New laws for short-term rentals were passed in May 2024. These laws will give counties more authority to enforce and amend short-term rental laws. The new law was set to take effect on January 1, 2025.

Consult local government resources or your legal counsel to stay compliant. Although the new law will affect the vacation rentals industry, the legislation itself will help address housing shortages by converting short-term rentals into long-term housing options for residents.

A quick call to the local Department of Planning can save you from a lot of headaches. They have records of each property's recorded type, and what's permitted and what's not. This is especially important in Hawaii, where unpermitted structures can lead to fines and/or big renovation bills.

Approach with Respect

One final piece of advice in this section: Remember that Hawaii is more than just a market. It's a special place with a history and culture unlike anywhere else in the world. The trauma that Hawaii went through in the past means skepticism is built into how natives approach businesspeople, and especially outsiders, so you have to be gentle. Smaller islands might be harder to break into. And you will stick out like a sore thumb if you approach property owners without respect and humility.

When you approach native Hawaiians about their properties, treat them like your family. Listen to the stories of the homeowners you're working with, and always aim to create win-win situations. Create deals that share wealth with the property owners, so they walk away with something rather than nothing, or worse, a foreclosure on their record. For me, that's what investing the Pono Way is all about—doing what's right for everyone involved.

When you lead with heart and stay Pono in how you handle deals, people notice. That kind of integrity builds your reputation—and sometimes, it even brings opportunities your way that you didn't see coming. My roots and mission are here in Hawaii, but I've also learned that keeping an open mind and being willing to grow can take you places you never imagined. That's how I ended up doing my first deal outside the islands.

Investing Beyond Hawaii

This book is about investing in Hawaii real estate, but sometimes opportunities come from places you'd never expect. For me, opportunity knocked in Oklahoma recently. Yeah, I know, sounds like a far cry from Hawaii, but let me share what I learned from my first out-of-state investment.

I was at a tax auction in Oklahoma, looking to pick up a property I could flip quickly. I didn't know a soul in the area, but my coaches gave me the green light, so I dove in. I bought a house sight unseen for $60,000. It seemed like a steal, but when I finally laid eyes on it, let's just say I wasn't prepared for what I saw. It was a completely burnt-down house. Yeah, you heard that right. The house was toast. Literally.

Now, if I were new to the game, that could've been the end of the story right there. But I didn't panic. I knew the land itself still held value, and I wasn't about to walk away from the deal. As we drove around the neighborhood, I noticed two brand-new houses down the street with For Sale signs. So I snapped a picture of one of the signs and called the number. It turned out that the realtor selling those homes was also a general contractor—exactly the type of person I would need if I was going to flip this house.

The next day, I met him to walk through my property. He gave me a detailed scope of work, and we struck a deal. From there, it was all about trust and teamwork. I managed the project remotely, wiring funds in stages from Hawaii as he and his crew worked through the renovations. By the end of it, I had put $200,000 into the house, bringing my total investment to $260,000. Once the house is finished, I expect it will sell for around $375,000 to $395,000. Not bad, right?

The key to success in out-of-state investing is having a solid team. You need people on the ground you can trust— realtors, contractors, inspectors—because you can't just hop on a plane every time something comes up. That's why relationships are everything in this business.

Looking back, this deal taught me a few things. First, always expect the unexpected. Second, even when things don't go as planned, there's usually a way to make it work if you're willing to put in the effort and think creatively. And third, which I feel like is the most important lesson—never let fear hold you back. Taking that leap into an unfamiliar market opened up a whole new world of possibilities for me.

So whether you're investing locally or out of state, the principles are the same. Do your homework, build your network, and stay adaptable. You never know where the next big opportunity might be waiting.

MAIN TAKEAWAYS FROM CHAPTER 7.2

1. **There are different ways to invest—pick the one that fits your goals.** Real estate investing isn't one-size-fits-all. You've got flips, new builds, wholesale deals, and more. Some strategies bring in quick cash, others build long-term wealth. The key is knowing your goals and choosing the strategy that gets you there the Pono Way.

2. **Every island in Hawaii is its own market.** Oahu isn't the same as Maui. The Big Island is different from Kauai. Each island has its own personality, price points, zoning rules, and buyer behaviors. What works on one island might flop on another. You've got to know the local market if you want to invest right.

3. **You've got to do your homework before every deal.** You can't skip the research. That means look into zoning, title history, comps, building permits—everything. A bad deal will sneak up on you if you don't know what you're looking for. When you do your due diligence, you protect yourself and the people you serve.

Chapter 7.3

Building a Dream Team

Real estate investing is the one thing that has helped me get my time back, and believe me, I've tried a lot of things. Investing in real estate is the only thing I've ever done that truly puts my money—and at first, other people's money—to work for me. One thing that really helped was connecting with the right people, including people who eventually became part of my business team. People come into your life for a reason. Some stay and some don't. It's the relationships you build and create that matter. I'm in it for the long haul, so building good relationships with people and finding the right members to add to my team are important to me.

Have you ever heard the phrase, "Your network is your net worth"? It's true. The person right next to you can bring an amazing amount of value to you and your real estate business, and you can also bring value to them by offering them opportunities to invest in a way that helps Hawaiians. You're often just one conversation away from the exact person you need to talk to to get the next deal rolling. You can use that to your advantage by talking to friends and family members who may have connections to the right people as you grow your business and build your Dream Team.

When you're first getting into real estate investing, you'll wear a lot of hats. If you follow the HUI Framework, your business will grow and you'll get your name out there. The deals will start coming to you, and you'll want to have a number of professionals on your contacts list. Eventually, you'll hire employees to really free up your time. Let's start with the outside professionals you need on your Dream Team and work our way to hiring paid staff. There are four main types of professionals you'll want to have professional connections with: acquirers, lenders, attorneys, and contractors.

ACQUIRERS

Acquirers, otherwise known as deal finders, are a position that will likely be headed up by you when you first get going, especially if you're starting out with little to no money. We're talking about directly approaching homeowners who haven't listed their properties with a realtor or wholesaler. You can find these homeowners by Driving for Dollars, cold calling, pulling pre-foreclosure lists through escrow companies, and posting on social media.

Social media is one of my favorite ways to connect with homeowners. All you do is put it out there that you're starting to invest and are looking for deals—just ask people to contact you if they know anyone who's looking to sell. You can also get a lot of leads by talking to people who are already in the industry like appraisers, escrow officers, or landscapers. You can also approach friends, family, and even the mailman. Another of my favorite strategies is going to network meetings that real estate investors and people in the industry attend. These are all free strategies I talk more about under the Finding Deals section of this chapter. There are other professionals you should connect with who can help you find deals, too. Let's talk about who you need to know that will make great potential Dream Team members.

Realtors

First up are realtors. They work directly with homeowners all the time. If a homeowner client wants to sell their property, the realtor will list it on a Multiple Listing Service (MLS) that's visible to the public. They also coordinate with other realtors to find buyers. As a real estate investor, having a realtor is super helpful because they will handle all the details and paperwork that come with the deal. But be careful—it's very important to find a realtor with experience dealing with investors. You want someone who understands the back-and-forth negotiation we need, because we want to get the best price on a property so we can flip or wholesale it and still make a profit.

Wholesalers

You will also want to connect with a wholesaler. If you choose wholesaling as your real estate strategy, a good wholesaler is your new best friend. Wholesalers find deals by talking to homeowners interested in selling their homes. Once they get the house under contract, they will assign the contract to you for a fee, usually somewhere in the neighborhood between $1,000 and $5,000.

Internal Team Members

As you get more experience and start making some money, you'll want to consider hiring an employee to help acquire properties. An internal acquisition team can save you time by scrubbing Craigslist, Facebook Marketplace, and the MLS for deals. Eventually, when you're established, opportunities will come to you.

LENDERS

You may need to secure the financing to purchase a deal, so the next professional you need on your Dream Team is a lender. I'm not a financial expert, so make sure you consult with your financial expert and tax professional to figure out what will work best for you.

There are many options to fund deals. And don't count out your network! You may be surprised who in your circle has money and may be interested in investing with you. Below are some of the most common lenders you'll want to make connections with for your Dream Team. I go into more detail on exactly how things work with funding in section 7.7 of this chapter.

Conventional Bank Loan Officers

Banks are some of the cheapest ways to get a loan to pay for a property or home because they offer lower interest rates. Set up an appointment with your bank's loan officer to find out what they may be able to make available to you. While you're there, talk to your mortgage lender to see if you qualify for a home equity line of credit (HELOC) against your home or another property you own. Many investors also use HELOCs to fund real estate deals.

Hard Money Lenders

Most investors use hard money lenders. Hard money lenders are companies and individuals offering short-term loans (anywhere from 6 to 18 months) for real estate investing. These lenders use the property as collateral and don't rely on personal or business credit scores.[1] Hard money lenders move quicker but also charge higher interest rates. Ask around to find out who the trustworthy hard money lenders are in your area, or look online at some of the top-rated hard money lenders, like HouseMax Funding, Easy Street Capital, or Express Capital Financing.

Private Money Lenders

A private money lender is someone who has money in their savings, in a home equity line of credit, life insurance, stocks, cryptocurrency, or in their self-directed retirement fund that they're looking to invest into your deals to get a higher return than they'd get in the stock market or other investment vehicle. A private money lender can be anyone—mom, dad, uncle, auntie, or someone else you come across. An example of this includes how my uncle used his self-directed IRA to invest in some real estate deals with me.

Seller Financing

Seller financing is where the homeowner becomes the bank by placing a mortgage against the property for the amount you want to buy it for. That means instead of going to a traditional bank for a loan, *you* make monthly payments directly to the seller—just like you would with a bank. You agree on a down payment, interest rate, and loan terms, and then it's all written into a promissory note and recorded like any other mortgage.

Now, this is where it can really work in your favor, especially in Hawaii. A lot of times, you'll come across families that own a property free and clear. They don't have a mortgage, and they don't necessarily want to sell to the first cash buyer waving a lowball offer. If you can show them a way to earn steady income every month while keeping some control over how the deal plays out, seller financing can be a win-win. Great places to find opportunities for seller financing are Craigslist and Facebook Marketplace—places where sellers list their property for sale by owner.

Investment Partners

Finding other investors to partner with is a great way to grow and scale your business. Especially if you're new, partnering with a seasoned investor can offer a wealth of information and be the key to opening doors you couldn't have opened on your own. But proceed with caution. Before you decide to partner with someone, do your research. Ask around to see if they're trusted in the industry. What other businesses do they own? How have they dealt with other investors in the past?

Insurance Brokers

If you have a whole life insurance policy, you can use that to fund deals. Talk to your broker to see how much cash value is in your policy and if that can be used for real estate investing.

Financial Advisors

Another great connection to make for your Dream Team is an investment or financial advisor. If you have a 401K, that can be used to fund deals. Your financial advisor can give you advice on how to leverage it for real estate investing.

TITLE/ESCROW OFFICER

The next professional you want is an investor-friendly title/escrow officer. This professional handles the legal and financial details of closing a property transaction. A good one will know how to do certain things most escrow officers don't, like double closings, or when you do two closings, back to back, on the same property. Ask for recommendations for an amazing title/escrow officer from people you trust in the real estate investment world.

CONTRACTORS

When it comes to real estate investing, it definitely pays to know a good contractor. Look for one with a good reputation who stands behind their work, even if they take a loss. You'll also want to make sure you have someone who is:

- Knowledgeable and motivated
- Shows up on time
- Budget-friendly
- Licensed and insured

In Hawaii, if you burn somebody, everyone will know because the islands are small and people talk. Ask family and friends, check the Department of Commerce and Consumer

Affairs, or ask around at construction sites and home improvement stores. Don't forget about the subcontractors, too—painters, roofers, framers, etc.

ATTORNEYS

Another great addition to your Dream Team is an attorney. If you plan on creating a business, they are an integral part in helping you separate and protect your personal assets from your business investments. Attorneys can also look at contracts and legal documents. They're a great resource to turn to when you have questions, and they can help draft contracts if you're a contractor or need contracts for your partnerships. They can also be a huge help with purchase and sales agreements.

When you're looking for an attorney experienced in real estate investing, ask for referrals from other investors, realtors, and escrow officers.

OTHER DREAM TEAM MEMBERS

We've covered the four main Dream Team categories, but that's not a complete list of people who can help you grow your business. Here are some other team members you may want to consider adding in the future.

- Lead Generation Specialists
- Social Media Managers
- Office and Administration Employees
- Surveyors
- Home Inspectors

- Architects
- Insurance Agents
- Appraisers
- Draftsmen
- Accountants or CPAs
- Property Managers

And the list goes on. Think about anyone you might need to know in your real estate investment dealings, then go out of your way to find and connect with them. You never know when you might need one of these amazing experts!

Once you have a team of professionals in your network, you're ready to get out there to start finding deals. In the next few sections of this chapter, you'll learn about how to find, analyze, fund, and close deals. Before we get into that, here's a quick breakdown of the stages of a deal, so you know what to expect each step of the way:

Step 1: Find a deal (See section 7.4)

Step 2: Analyze the deal for multiple strategies (See section 7.5)

Step 3: Make an offer (See section 7.6)

Step 4: Offer is accepted

Step 5: Put down an earnest money deposit (EMD), usually 1% of the purchase price

Step 6: J-1 Inspection Period 14 days

Step 7: Start Sourcing Funds (See section 7.7)

MAIN TAKEAWAYS FROM CHAPTER 7.3

1. **You can't build a real estate business alone. You need a team.** This isn't a solo mission. You'll need the right people around you—contractors, realtors, lenders, inspectors, and more. The sooner you start building your Dream Team, the smoother your projects will run and the faster you'll grow.

2. **Work with people who share your values.** It's not only about skill—it's about trust and alignment. You want to work with people who understand the Pono Way, who treat clients and communities with respect, and who are in the real estate game for the long game, not just quick cash.

3. **Your team will grow as your business grows.** At first, you might only have a few key people helping out. That's okay. As you take on more deals, your team will naturally expand. Focus on finding solid, dependable folks early on—so you can all grow together.

Chapter 7.4

Finding Deals

Let's cut to the bottom line. You have goals for your future, and you want to know if finding real estate deals in Hawaii will help you achieve them. To figure that out, let's look at other people who have become Hawaii real estate investors before you. I can't promise you'll make money—that depends on how much action you take—but knowing how things have worked out for others will give you an idea of what could be possible for you.

The average annual income of real estate investors in Hawaii is $129,328 according to ZipRecruiter.[1] Keep in mind, that's just the average and includes everyone who describes themselves as a real estate investor, whether they know what they're doing or not. When you have a roadmap like the one in this book, you'll get results faster with fewer mistakes and missteps. Even if you don't want to make real estate investing your full-time career right away, it can help provide additional income—even passive income month after month if you get into rentals—above and beyond what you're used to, without having to use your own money.

So let's talk about it. The number one question I am always asked about deals is: Where do I find them? The great thing about Hawaii is there are deals everywhere, which means there are plenty to go around. This section of the HUI Framework is all about the different ways you can find deals, from free strategies to paid—and everything in between. I've pretty much done them all!

ON- AND OFF-MARKET DEALS

There are two types of deals you can look for—on-market and off-market deals. Properties listed for sale are considered on-market deals. Off-market deals are *not* publicly listed for sale. They may require more time and effort to find and negotiate, but you can often get them cheaper and with less competition because you're going directly to the property owner.

No matter what kind of deal you pursue, it's important to consider who might be a motivated seller. These are people who are ready and willing to sell due to life circumstances, like a divorce, a family emergency, or a new job. Other motivated sellers include people who want to free up cash for an investment opportunity, those who inherit a property they don't want, or owners struggling to afford their property due to a change in tax laws.

Although it might be easier to obtain a deal from motivated sellers, remember to look out for their interests, too. It's the Pono Way. Make sure you're the best solution, and if not, refer them to someone who is. Keep reading to learn more about my favorite ways to find on- and off-market deals.

Driving for Dollars

Have some wheels and a tank of gas? Hop in the car and do some drive-arounds—I call these Driving for Dollars—and you'll see potential deals. Before I had a network of developers and listing agents, this was one of my favorite ways to find deals. I'd just drive around neighborhoods, taking note of any homes that looked run-down or empty. Every time I saw a place that looked beat up, I'd jot down the address. Then when I got home, I'd look up the owner and reach out. Sometimes I'd just sit with them and listen to their story to see if they'd be open to selling.

By going directly to the owners, I found opportunities that big investors missed or just didn't bother with. It's a slower approach, but I believe in keeping things personal. I put in the work myself, right here in the community. That's how I built my reputation: I am known as someone who respects the land and the people. I'm not just looking to make a quick buck—I really want to help local families hold onto a piece of home.

Writing Letters

Another low-cost way to find deals is writing letters. I get a hold of a tax map key, choose a street, then write down the addresses of all the properties on that street. Then I do a public records search to find the names of the property owners. Next, I write a personal letter saying something like, "Hey, my name is Fuzzy Jardine. I see you have a property on 123 Main Street. I'm a local, born and raised, and I'm looking to purchase in the area. If you're interested in selling, please give me a call." Then I put my business card inside the envelope with the letter and mail it out.

All this costs me is a bit of time and a stamp! If you stay consistent, this method works. I found I would land a deal anywhere from 1–5% of the properties I mailed to. If you want to be more direct and text or call, you can sometimes find their phone number if you have their name and address by using TruePeopleSearch.com.

Door Knocking and Cold Calling/Texting

Hand in hand with writing letters and Driving for Dollars are door knocking and cold calling or texting. Once you have people's contact information, you can partner up your letters with a personal visit, phone call, or text. You don't need an elaborate speech or script. Simply introduce yourself, tell them why you're contacting them, and see where the conversation goes.

Bandit Signs

Part of finding deals is learning how to attract them to you. The first thing you have to do is get the word out that you're looking, but you don't have to get fancy about it. In the early days, I put up bandit signs—those temporary plant-it-in-the-dirt-and-go roadside signs. I was straight to the point, local style. Bandit signs are cheap, but you'll want to make sure you don't put them up in areas where they're not allowed. Check city ordinances for the area you want to place signs.

Craigslist Ads

I used the same local-style message and took out Craigslist ads that said, "Fuzzy Buys Houses in Cash" with my number. This simple message was effective at reaching property owners who needed a quick, hassle-free sale. It wasn't long before developers and folks with properties they were considering selling started reaching out. Those ads connected me to some great deals, stuff that wasn't even listed. I wasn't competing with a bunch of other buyers, and that made a huge difference. Like I said before, this is like fishing in a secret spot only you know about.

A Craigslist ad was actually how I became a real estate developer. I placed an ad saying I was interested in purchasing property with cash and could close quickly. A real estate developer saw the ad and contacted me. It was perfect because I was looking for deals, and he had a deal and was looking for funds. I was able to bring the money to the table because I was part of a network of investors.

Foreclosure Auctions

Another great way to find deals that aren't on the market is attending foreclosure auctions. A foreclosure auction was actually my business partner, Zasha Smith's, first deal. If you're not familiar with foreclosure and foreclosure auctions, here's how it all works.

A property may go into foreclosure if a homeowner stops making payments on their mortgage. Many loans go into default after 90 days, and if the property owner doesn't catch up on payments or make steps to negotiate with the lender, the lender may take ownership of the property and sell it at auction to recover their losses.

If the lender decides to pursue foreclosure and sell it at auction, the property is listed publicly through a Notice of Trustee's Sale or Notice of Foreclosure Sale and advertised in local papers or online. You can visit the county website or the courthouse and ask to view pre-foreclosure lists. Escrow companies and real estate agents are great places to get these lists, too.

Anyone can attend a foreclosure auction. Sometimes there's even an open house where you can see a property first, but not always. Once the auction starts, prospective buyers bid on the property, and the winning bidder typically must pay in full immediately or within a short time frame. Most foreclosure auctions don't allow financing, so be prepared to pay in cash or with certified funds.

After the auction, the winner takes possession of the property as-is, and you're responsible for any unpaid taxes, second mortgages, and liens. Tenants may also become the winner's responsibility if the property is a rental. You can get some really great deals at foreclosure auctions, as property often goes for below market value. But, as with any deal, you really need to do your research first, so you can avoid overbidding or getting stuck with expensive repairs or renovations you didn't plan for.

Short Sales

A short sale in real estate occurs when a homeowner sells their property for less than the amount owed on their mortgage.

This often happens when the homeowner is struggling financially and unable to make mortgage payments, and the property's market value has dropped below the outstanding loan balance. The homeowner wants to avoid foreclosure and negative impacts on their credit, so they choose to sell the property at a loss.

On the other end of this kind of deal is the lender. When there's an outstanding mortgage, the lender must agree to accept less than what is owed on the mortgage to avoid the more costly and time-consuming foreclosure process. This can lead to a great deal under market value for you, but negotiations can be complicated, and these types of deals can take a while to go through, despite the name being "short sale."

Connecting with Professionals

You know how they say, "It's not just WHAT you know, it's WHO you know"? That's 100% true when it comes to finding real estate deals. When you make connections with the right people, it pays off. Next, I'm going to share the types of people you will want to build your Dream Team with.

Realtors and Real Estate Agents. Get to know your local real estate agents. They can comb through the Multiple Listing Service and find deals to fit your specifications. The MLS has a wide variety of listings with property information and access to market data, but on-market listings tend to be competitive and harder to get for below-market costs.

Other Investors. Not every deal is a good fit for every investor. Don't be afraid to talk to other investors about deals. You never know when they come across one they can pass on to you.

Listing Agents. Find out who the listing agents in your area are and ask them about the pocket listings—off-market deals agents keep in their back pockets to share with select buyers they trust—or properties that have been on the market for a while.

Make it known to all your connections what types of properties you're interested in, so they can keep an eye out for you. For example, let's say you're looking for properties in Pukalani for less than $500,000. You don't mind if a property needs work, and you're willing to close within 30 days. Tell the realtors and listing agents in that area, and they can bring to your attention any properties that fit the bill. When things come across their desk, they can let you know. You never know when someone will pass on something that wasn't a good fit for them.

Who you need to connect with also depends on your chosen Hawaii real estate market. There are pros and cons to each market, as I previously outlined in this chapter, and each market has its own circle of helpful connections.

Social Media and Craigslist

Here's a quick ninja tip—don't forget to regularly peruse Craigslist and Facebook Marketplace to find For Sale By Owner properties. Social media has a wide reach, and it offers great networking opportunities, too. I've used social media to find several deals while I was scrolling. I've even paid my earnest money deposit online, then closed the deal later through an escrow company. And don't forget to join Facebook groups. There are tons of them for people looking to sell property or network with property sellers. These groups are great because people share knowledge and information. You just have to realize you don't have much control over *what* information people share with you.

Wholesalers

Connecting with wholesalers is another great strategy for finding deals. They do a lot of the leg work it takes to look for deals off-market and get them under contract. Then they look for investors like you to sell the contracts for a small assignment fee. When you work with wholesalers, you can make quick profits without investing in the property itself, but you will need strong negotiation skills.

Tax Auctions

In Hawaii, if people don't pay their land tax, the property gets auctioned off. Usually, the property owner is given two or three years to pay their taxes. If they don't, the property is put up for auction. At tax deed auctions, anyone can attend and put in an offer. If the offer is accepted, the person who made the offer gets the tax deed. Sometimes you can get tax deed auction properties for pennies on the dollar. There are some rules and regulations that are important to know, and we go deep into this strategy inside HUI Mastermind.

There is potential for excellent deals for investors with cash on hand, especially for those who attend tax deed auctions. But these auctions can be risky because information on the properties tends to be limited.

MAIN TAKEAWAYS FROM CHAPTER 7.4

1. **Deals are everywhere—you just need to know where and how to look.** Many people think there are no deals left in Hawaii, but that's not true. You have to know where to look and how to think creatively. Whether it's Driving for Dollars, working with agents, or tapping into your network, opportunities are out there if you're willing to put in the effort.

2. **Your network is one of your best deal-finding tools.** Sometimes your next deal won't come from a listing—it'll come from a conversation. Let people know what you do. The more people you talk to, the more likely it is that someone will say, "Hey, I know a person who needs to sell."

3. **Marketing doesn't have to be fancy to be effective.** You don't need a massive ad budget to start finding deals. Simple things like bandit signs, social media posts, and word of mouth can go a long way. Just be consistent and clear about how you help people, and leads will start to come in.

4. **The best deals help everyone involved.** When you find a deal where the seller gets relief and the buyer gets value— you've found a Pono deal. That's the kind of investing that builds a strong business and solid reputation.

Chapter 7.5

Analyzing Deals

How do you decide what's a good deal and what's not?

It depends on how much income you make now and how much risk you're willing to take on. If you're new, you want to look for properties where you will have a higher profit margin. This is especially important in the first few deals, when unexpected things tend to pop up. If you end up going over the budget for renovations, or something isn't up to code and needs to be fixed in a building project, you need larger profit margins so you won't be upside down.

I learned this lesson the hard way on my very first deal—the one I told you about in the first chapter. I worked with another student, and together we set up an arrangement to take over mortgage payments for an elderly woman living alone in a big house on the Big Island. What I didn't mention was what happened after that.

I was managing the project, doing everything from coordinating the repairs to handling any unexpected building costs that crept up. I had my coaches and partners supporting me on the financial end, but I was the one there on-site, overseeing the entire project. It wasn't easy—costs ended up running higher than we'd expected. But by the end, all the hard work paid off, and I still walked away with $12,000 from that first deal.

That moment was huge for me. I had proven to myself I could do this, that the knowledge I'd gained was real, and even though the profit margin was narrower than I expected, all the hours spent learning the ropes were worth it. My first deal wasn't just about the cash—it was the start of a path that let me build something for myself and my family, all while helping others along the way.

Today, I love teaching new real estate investors how to analyze deals. I want to make sure they know what to look for so their first deals go well. Inside the HUI Mastermind, Zasha and I physically walk students through properties so they can learn what to look for in real property situations. I can't physically walk with you through a property in this book, but I will show you how to use the HUI Framework to analyze deals the Pono Way, so you can identify good deals the same way our HUI Academy and Mastermind students do.

When you analyze deals, the goal is to make sure it will be a good investment. You also want to identify properties that will have a good outcome for everyone—you and the property owner. You want to make a profit while keeping in mind the needs of native Hawaiians, and if you can do that, everyone wins. When it comes to analyzing deals, I like to keep things simple. I'm what you'd call the "Flintstone" of the group because I lean on the basics when researching properties—multiplication, addition, subtraction, and division—so make sure to grab your calculator when analyzing properties!

Step 1: Start with the Purchase Price

Once you've used one of the deal-finding strategies I mentioned earlier to find potential investment properties, determine what you'll need to pay to purchase the property.

Step 2: Find Comparables and Determine the ARV

After that, you'll want to do a Comparative Market Analysis (CMA) by comparing properties similar to the one you want to purchase, in the area, that have recently sold. Bring in a real estate agent to find some comparable properties (also called comps) that have recently sold in the area. Then, hire a professional appraiser to assess the property's potential After Repair Value (ARV). The ARV is the estimated value of the property after you've fixed it up, and it's hugely important. An appraiser can also give you suggestions on which renovations to make, so that you can add value to the property.

Step 3: Estimate Renovation and Repair Costs

Next, you want to determine how much the renovations and repairs might cost. It is your goal to make sure there will be enough room to make the numbers work after renovation costs. When you're looking to rehab a property, follow these steps to make sure you have a good estimate of renovations and repairs.

First, walk through the property with a contractor to identify all necessary repairs and improvements needed.

Your contractor can give estimates for labor and materials and help you make a budget. Here's a pro tip: Always get three quotes from different contractors, so you can compare pricing and timelines. Make sure to create a 10%–15% buffer (also called a contingency fund) for your rehab budget to cover unexpected expenses. You'll be glad you did!

Also, be sure to consult with a home inspector. They can catch things you and your contractor might miss, and that can save you big bucks or even help you negotiate a better purchase price.

Another professional you'll want on hand is a project manager to oversee daily tasks and ensure everything stays on schedule and within budget. You'll also want an architect or designer to help plan and design the renovations. Ask around and read reviews—you want somebody you can really trust.

Step 4: Determine Other Fees

Whether it's private money, hard money, or a bank loan, you'll need to account for lender fees like origination fees (the cost to process a new loan application), interest rates, and closing costs. And don't forget to factor in the time it takes to complete the deal. Your strategy here depends on what you're doing with the property. If you're flipping, hard money or private money might be your best bet because it's faster. For a rental with minimal repairs, a conventional loan might make more sense. I break down the different types of funding in more detail in the Funding section of this chapter.

One thing you can't skip is insurance. Trust me, I learned that the hard way. One time, my partner forgot to insure a project we were working on. Next thing we knew, part of the house got burned, and we had to shell out extra money to fix it. Lesson learned. Always get insurance. You'll also want to estimate taxes, utilities, and other carrying costs. You can usually look up property taxes online and get estimates for utilities and insurance from providers.

Step 5: Calculate Potential Profit

Now that you have all the numbers, it's time to get out the calculator and start punching buttons. Add up the following numbers to estimate the amount you can expect to put into the property before selling or renting it out:

Purchase Price + Cost of Repairs/Renovations +
Financing Fees + Insurance + Taxes + Utilities
= **Estimated Total Input**

To determine if the deal will be profitable, you'll subtract the Estimated Total Input from the ARV, like this:

ARV - Estimated Total Input = **Estimated Profit**

If there's a decent gap between the total input and the ARV—and I'm talking anywhere between $60k to $200k in potential profit—it's a green light to proceed. If the gap is smaller, I recommend you keep searching for a better deal.

Step 6: Create an Exit Strategy (or Two)

Even if you do all the calculations and things look great, not every deal will go exactly to plan. Make sure you have some exit strategies to help you finish the deal with a win—no matter what. Think about how you could switch strategies if you need to. You could wholesale the deal, fix-and-flip it, or rent it out and refinance it. Having multiple options gives you flexibility if things don't go as planned.

For example, you might intend to wholesale a property, but if it doesn't sell, you could pivot to fixing and flipping. Or, if the market shifts, you might decide to hold onto it as a rental. At the end of the day, the homework you do upfront is where the money's made. If you buy right, you're setting yourself up to win when it's time to cash out.

BEYOND FINDING DEALS

There will always be real estate deals to be had. This book may be about real estate investing in Hawaii, but no matter what country, state, or city you're in, everyone needs a roof over their heads. Getting your first deal may seem difficult, but once you've done it, doing it again gets easier. Plus, you're holding the blueprint to real estate investing the Pono Way—the HUI Framework—in your hands right now. That means you can skip all the wondering about what to do and where to start. Everything you need to know to find, analyze, and fund deals is right here.

But it's not only about knowing what to do—you actually have to DO it. If you refuse to take action, you won't produce any results. So, commit to taking action and putting the time and effort into learning what to do—and then do it. You can become a millionaire in the first year if you put the time into real estate investing and take action. Even if this is a side hustle for you right now, if you consistently follow the HUI Framework and start your real estate adventure, you can become a millionaire in three to five years.

MAIN TAKEAWAYS FROM CHAPTER 7.5

1. **If the numbers don't work, it's not a deal.** Don't fall in love with a property just because it has potential. You've got to run the numbers—find out about repair costs, holding costs, and resale value to determine the profit margin. If the math doesn't make sense, walk away. The numbers always tell the truth.

2. **Know your exit strategy before you buy.** Are you flipping, renting, or wholesaling? Your plan for the property should shape how you analyze it. Different strategies have different risk levels, timelines, and profit margins—so don't move forward without a clear exit in mind.

3. **Always overestimate expenses and underestimate profits.** Things go wrong. Contractors run late. Materials cost more. The last thing you want is to be stuck in a deal that barely breaks even—or worse, loses money. Give yourself some margin from the start, so you're protected if something doesn't go according to plan.

4. **A good deal is one that helps everyone and keeps you in business.** You can make money and still do it the right way. The best deals are where the seller gets help, the buyer gets value, and you get paid. That's how you keep your reputation strong and your business growing the Pono Way.

Chapter 7.6

Making Offers

You've found and analyzed some deals and are ready to take the next step: making offers. That's the exciting part, right? There are several ways to make offers. The method you use depends on what kind of deal it is—on-market or off-market. I'll walk you through how I do an on-market deal first, then an off-market deal.

On-Market Offers

If you're working on an on-market deal, I recommend making your offer through a real estate agent. Most on-market properties are listed on the MLS, which allows real estate agents to create an email alert based on what a person is looking for. When I'm searching for deals on the MLS, I ask my agent to set me up on an email list based on my specifications, whether that means finding fixer-uppers or properties in specific neighborhoods. Once I start getting daily or weekly emails, I'll pick the ones that catch my eye. Then I start the ball rolling by telling my agent, "Hey, let's put in an offer."

I always make the initial offer below the asking price. It's all part of the negotiation game and leaves room for the seller to counter. If an offer is accepted, I check the property with my agent to make sure everything lines up, and the process is pretty straightforward from there. Once an offer is accepted, you enter into a contract. This contract usually includes an inspection period of 7–14 days, where you can bring in a contractor or home inspector to make sure the deal makes sense and there are no unwanted surprises that will kill profitability. The inspection period gives you an out, just in case—so if the sellers ask you to waive the inspection, that's a no go.

Off-Market Offers

I also work off-market deals where I connect directly with the homeowners. These are the types of deals I find by driving through local neighborhoods. I search for properties that look like they need work, with overgrown yards, sagging roofs, that sort of thing. First, I knock on the door and introduce myself. This starts a relationship with the property owner. "Aloha, I'm Fuzzy Jardine. I'm buying properties in the area. Have you ever thought about selling?" It's a simple conversation starter. I'm not pushy. I'm just letting them know I'm interested and asking if they or anyone they know might be looking to sell.

For off-market leads, I also use paid lists, like pre-foreclosure lists or properties owned by out-of-state landlords. These lists often highlight motivated sellers. When I call, I keep it straightforward. "Hi, I'm Fuzzy, a local home buyer. Are you interested in selling your property?" I never come across as intrusive or mention how I found them. The goal is to open up a conversation, understand their situation, and see if I can help solve their problem. If I can't, I'll refer them to a lender or help them find creative solutions to their problems.

These conversations are the start of negotiating. Negotiating directly with homeowners is all about listening. I'll sit down with them, walk through the property to get a feel for the property's value, and ask some tough but necessary questions—like how much they owe on their mortgage or what they think their property is worth. I want to understand the seller's motivations. Often, people overestimate, thinking their home is worth way more than it is. That's when I show them comparable homes that have sold in the area and explain the reality of the market. My goal isn't to take advantage of them, but to instead find a win-win solution.

If the property looks promising, I make sure to do my homework beforehand. I run the numbers like I described in the Analyzing Deals section of this chapter, and I determine what I'd need to offer to make it a deal. When I meet with the homeowner the next time, I'm ready to discuss fair terms based on their situation and the property's condition. Along every step of the negotiation, I make sure I'm communicating clearly, concisely, and respectfully. I'm also willing to compromise on certain terms to reach a mutually beneficial agreement—I want that win-win solution!

The Purchase Contract

For off-market deals, having a purchase contract ready is

key. Consult with your real estate lawyer to create one. The purchase contract is a legally binding agreement between the buyer and seller that outlines the terms of the property sale. Inside the contract, you'll find a description with the details of the property being sold. It also lists the purchase price and any contingencies or conditions that must be met for the sale to proceed, like financing or a property inspection. Then you'll see the closing date when the property transfer will be finalized and a place for signatures from the buyer and seller. I always keep a stack of contracts that my lawyer helped me create on hand. If a seller is ready to move forward, we fill it out on the spot, take a picture, and send it to escrow with an earnest money deposit. That makes it official.

Final Words on Making Offers

There are a few strategies I like to use to move a negotiation forward if it seems to be stalling. But I only use them if it's going to create a good outcome for everyone—that's the Pono Way. The first strategy is urgency. Sometimes I'll create a time-sensitive offer to motivate sellers who need to close quickly. The second strategy is straight up making a cash offer. Cash equals speed and certainty for the seller, and it's a great way to strengthen your offer.

Remember, this is all a numbers game. You've got to make a lot of offers, sometimes hundreds, before you find the right deal. Don't get discouraged. The key is to stay consistent and keep putting yourself out there. It will help you stay motivated to remember that every "no" gets you closer to a "yes."

MAIN TAKEAWAYS FROM CHAPTER 7.6

1. **Making offers is a numbers game—so make a lot of offers.** Too many people wait for the "perfect" deal to fall in their lap. Don't do that. The more offers you make, the more chances you have to get a "yes." Real investors regularly make offers, even on deals that don't look perfect at first glance.

2. **Don't be afraid to offer less than the asking price.** Sellers expect negotiation. If the numbers don't work for you, make the offer that *does*. Your job isn't to pay retail—it's to find a price that gives you room to do the needed work, make a profit, and help the seller move on.

3. **Use formulas, not feelings.** Never guess or go off a gut feeling when writing offers. Make sure you're making smart, profitable decisions. Stick to the math, and you'll protect yourself every time.

4. **Make your offer a win for everyone involved.** When you present your offer, explain how it helps the seller. Maybe it gives them peace of mind, a fresh start, or a way out of foreclosure. When you lead with empathy and clarity, even a lower offer can feel like the best option to the property owner in need.

Chapter 7.7

Funding Deals

You know, a lot of people think you need a pile of money to get started in real estate, but that's just not true. The secret is finding the deal first. If you lock down a good deal, the money will come—guaranteed.

I learned this when I was getting started. I didn't have much money, but I knew how to hustle. I started putting up ads on Craigslist saying I was looking for properties. That's how I connected with developers who needed funding. At the same time, I tapped into my coaching network to find investors who had money but didn't want the hassle of managing a project. I became the middleman who brought the deals to the developers and connected them with the investors. We'd close the deals and split the profits. You don't need to be rich—you just need to know how to find a deal and then put the pieces together.

The bottom line is this: Stop worrying about having money. Focus on finding good deals. If you bring a solid deal to the table, there's always someone out there ready to fund it. That's how I got started, and that's how I teach my students to succeed, too.

There are three main types of funding for real estate deals—typical bank funding, typical investor funding, and creative funding. Before getting an offer accepted, you should have some things in place and know what type of financing you're going to use, so decisions about funding don't slow down the process. In this section of the chapter, I'm going to talk about the different ways you can get started funding real estate deals. I'll share some of my personal stories and what worked for me and my business partner, Zasha. I'm not a financial expert, so make sure you talk to a financial advisor and tax professional to figure out what the best options are for you specifically.

Working With Sellers

When working with sellers, you want to have some crucial conversations first to avoid miscommunications or roadblocks that could slow or kill the deal later. Here are some things you'll need to ask them about.

First, find out what their financial situation is like. Do they need money right now? Are they looking for a lump sum or ongoing cash flow? How much do they really want out of this deal? Are they flexible on terms?

Next, find out what their motivation for selling is. Are they a tired landlord looking for cash flow? In poor health and can't care for their property anymore? Maybe they inherited a home they don't want to keep. Knowing the "why" behind their desire to sell can help you create a win-

win for everyone. Then, find out their timeline. How soon do they want to make things happen?

Finally, find out what their current mortgage figures are. Is it paid off? If not, what's their interest rate? Do they have any liens on it? How much do they pay in taxes and insurance? Do they generate any cash flow from the property with rentals? These questions will help you see the entire picture.

TYPICAL BANK FUNDING OPTIONS

Cash

Cash is king, and if you've got it, that is certainly the fastest, easiest way to fund real estate deals. If you have a substantial amount of available cash, you can pay for properties outright without going through the loan process or searching out partnerships. Property is expensive, though, especially here in Hawaii, so you may need to look into other sources of funding. If cash is the way you want to go, find real estate agents who understand how cash buying works. This will help the whole process move smoothly and quickly.

Conventional Bank Loans

Like I said in section 7.3 of this chapter, banks are some of the cheapest ways to finance deals because conventional banks offer lower interest rates. When I first got started, my wife and I applied for a bank loan. They looked at our W-2s, and we were able to qualify for a loan with a 4% interest rate. (Interest rates will differ according to what the Fed dictates at any given time, so check your establishment.)

Although interest rates tend to be lower at a personal bank, if you plan to apply for a bank loan, come ready because they require a lot of information like bank statements and back tax information. This whole process can be time-consuming and can take anywhere from 45 to 90 days. That doesn't always work for real estate investors because sometimes we need to move quicker than that. Set up an appointment with your bank's loan officer to find out what they can offer you.

Home Equity Line of Credit
A home equity line of credit, or HELOC, involves funds the bank lets you borrow against the value of your property. If you've got equity built up in a property you already own, you can tap into it to fund your deals. You can use that money however you need, whether it's for a down payment, renovations, or even closing costs. This is a great way to leverage the assets you already have to grow your portfolio.

TYPICAL INVESTOR FUNDING

Hard Money Loans
Many real estate investors use hard money lenders. Hard money lenders move more quickly, but they also charge higher interest rates. At the writing of this book, interest rates range from 10%–15% from hard money lenders, depending on your experience level. They also charge points or additional interest rate percentages at closing, which usually fall between one to three points. For example, let's say you borrow $100,000 from a hard money lender at 12% interest and an additional two points. The points could cost

you an additional several thousand dollars on top of the borrowed amount.

There are a few things you need to know about hard money lenders. First, they secure their money by having a first lien position against the home, meaning they have the right to foreclose on borrowers who don't pay them back. Second, hard money lenders don't like to work with new investors. They prefer to lend to investors with five to ten deals under their belts within 18–24 months. You may need to partner with another investor who has already proven they have enough experience to qualify to work with a hard money lender.

If you can find a hard money lender willing to give you a chance, even if you're a newbie, they typically lend anywhere from 75%–80% of the purchase price of the property and fund 100% of the construction. But be aware—they don't just give you all the money up front. They expect you to have some money in your account to fund the first phases of the project, like the demo and the framing, and then they give you a draw. In cases like that, another funding source is required for the down payment and first phases of the project.

One more super important thing to know about hard money companies is the difference between Dutch loans and non-Dutch loans. With a Dutch loan, you start paying interest on the full loan amount immediately after closing. For example, if you borrow $100,000, you're paying interest on the entire $100,000 from day one, even if you haven't used it all yet. On the other hand, with a non-Dutch loan, you only pay interest on the amount you actually draw. So, if you're approved for $100,000 but only pull $20,000 to start, you'll only pay interest on that $20,000. That's why I usually prefer non-Dutch loans. They give you flexibility and help you save on interest while your project is ramping up.

Another thing I look for in a hard money company is whether they wrap interest payments into the loan upfront. This means all interest payments are bundled into the loan at closing. While you might need to bring more money to the closing table in this kind of situation, you won't have to worry about making monthly interest payments because it's all taken care of until the loan is due. For me, it's worth the peace of mind and convenience of not having to remember to pay interest every month. Make sure you ask around, with people you trust for referrals, to find reputable hard lenders.

Private Money Lending

My favorite lender type is a private money lender—an individual with money in savings, a home equity line of credit, or retirement fund. Private money lenders want to invest in real estate deals because they can get a higher return on their investment than they'd get elsewhere, like the stock market. Working with a private money lender is great for you, too. Unlike hard money lending, where the lender sets the interest and points based on your experience, you and the private money lender can set your own interest rate and negotiate your own terms. A lien secures the loan against the property. The terms of the loan can be set up to incur interest that does not need to be paid until the property sells. Like hard money, private money can come in a lot faster, sometimes even that same day, enabling you to move quickly and close a deal in short order.

Private money lenders can be easier to find than you think. You can connect with private money lenders by posting on social media, attending networking meetings, and chatting up everyday people you meet in the elevator. I'm always ready with my five-second elevator pitch to let people know, "Hey, I help people gain double-digit returns on their money that's just sitting in the bank." Remember, private money can come from anyone—mom, dad, uncle, auntie, or someone else in your network—so don't overlook your personal connections.

Zasha's first private lenders found her on Instagram. In 2020, she was Driving for Dollars and posting that she was looking for deals as a beginning investor. Meanwhile, because of the pandemic, two experienced real estate investors had decided to stop fixing and flipping properties themselves. They were looking to leverage profits they had previously made, saw Zasha's post, and reached out. It was her first time getting private money and their first time lending. They met over dinner, and she negotiated to borrow $560,000 for the purchase and renovation of a property. It covered all her costs, and she ended up putting zero money into the deal.

I have a similar story of finding private lenders on social media. I reached out to a network of investors in a group I was part of on Facebook and showed them an opportunity they could fund profitably. They funded the project, and we secured their money by creating a mortgage deed, just like a bank, and filing it with the Bureau of Conveyances.

I managed the project with a developer, and we all made a good split of the profit at the end.

Partnerships

Finding other investors to partner with is a great way to grow and scale your business, especially if you're new and partner with a more experienced investor. A seasoned investor can be a wealth of information for you and the key to opening doors you couldn't have opened on your own. But proceed with caution. Before you decide to partner with someone, do your research. Ask around to see if they're trusted in the industry. Ask: What other businesses do they own? How have they dealt with other investors?

Proof of Funding

If you're planning to use a bank, private money, or hard money to fund a deal, there are a few things you need to have ready before your offer gets accepted. One of the most important things to have is proof of funds. This is a document or letter that shows you have the money available to purchase the property. This is what we call a cash offer.

Now, not every seller will require it, but having proof of funds can make your offer stand out, especially in competitive markets. Sometimes, my agent will even ask me for a screenshot of my bank account, so they can show the seller I'm serious.

If you're just starting out and don't have the funds yourself, no problem. You can work with a hard money lender or partner who does. They can provide the proof of funds you need, either with a letter or a bank statement screenshot.

CREATIVE FUNDING SOURCES

Subject-to Financing

Let me tell you about "subject-to" financing. It's one of those strategies in real estate that can really open doors, especially if you're looking to get creative with how you structure deals. When you buy a property subject-to, you're taking over the existing mortgage the seller already has in place. The loan stays in the seller's name, but you take control of the property and make the payments moving forward. Think of it as stepping into their shoes without having to go through the hassle of applying for a new loan yourself.

Why would a seller agree to this? Well, maybe they're struggling to make payments, or they're in a tough spot like a pre-foreclosure situation. They might want to get out from under the property and avoid damaging their credit with a foreclosure. For them, it's a way to walk away clean. For you, it's a way to acquire a property with little to no money down.

First, you'll negotiate with the seller and agree on terms. They agree to let you take over the mortgage, and you agree to make the payments. (I'll talk more about back payments that might be due in a few paragraphs.) Next, with the help of a titling agency, the title transfers to you. You now own the property, but the mortgage itself stays in the seller's name. Once that happens, it's now your responsibility to make those mortgage payments. If you don't, the seller's credit gets hit—so this method is all about trust and being reliable.

There are a few key things to keep in mind with subject-to financing. First, the bank that holds the loan technically has the right to call the loan due if they find out the property was sold. This is called the due-on-sale clause. But in most cases, as long as the payments are being made on time, banks don't usually make a fuss about it because they're not in the business of owning houses. They mainly care that the mortgage is paid.

Second, you've got to make sure the numbers work. Before taking over a mortgage, you need to know what the monthly payments are and whether the payments include insurance and property tax fees. You also need to find out if there are any back payments owed, and whether the deal makes sense for you in terms of cash flow or resale potential.

The subject-to financing strategy is great because it allows you to get into a property without needing a ton of cash or qualifying for a loan. It's also an excellent way to help a motivated seller while adding to your portfolio. But like anything in real estate, it takes doing your homework, being clear with the seller, and having a solid exit strategy in place. If you play it smart, subject-to financing can be a real game changer. It's definitely another tool to have in your investor toolkit.

Seller Financing

Let me break down seller financing for you—it's one of those strategies that can make deals happen when traditional financing just doesn't cut it. This is a simple concept: Instead of going through a bank, the seller becomes your lender.

Here's how it works. Say you find a property, and the seller owns it outright or has enough equity to leverage so that they can create a way to work with you. Instead of you getting a loan from the bank, the seller agrees to "finance" the sale for you. You and the seller work out the terms, like the down payment, interest rate, and monthly payments, and you start paying them directly. They hold the loan, which is called a "note." And you take over the property.

Why would a seller go for this? A lot of reasons. Maybe they want to sell the property quickly but still generate income from it. This strategy helps the seller avoid the big tax hit that comes with a lump sum sale because they're spreading the payments over time. Or maybe they like the idea of earning interest on the deal instead of putting their money in the bank. For you as the buyer, seller financing can be a game changer. You don't have to jump through hoops with a bank, and it's much more flexible. For example, you might negotiate a lower down payment, a better interest rate, or even skip all the credit checks.

Here's an example. Let's say you find a property worth $200,000. The seller agrees to finance it for you with a $20,000 down payment and a 5% interest rate on the remaining $180,000. You sign an agreement, the property title transfers to you, and you start making monthly payments to the seller. No banks, no hard money lenders. It's just you and the seller working together.

Now, like any other deal, you've got to run the numbers and make sure it makes sense. Know what the property is worth, what kind of cash flow you'll have, and if you can realistically make those payments. And, of course, get everything in writing—have a lawyer or escrow company handle the paperwork and use a title company to transfer the title to ensure both sides are protected.

Seller financing is a great tool for investors, especially when dealing with motivated sellers or properties that might not qualify for traditional loans. It's all about being creative and finding ways to make the deal work for everyone involved—the Pono Way.

Great places to find opportunities for seller financing are Craigslist and Facebook Marketplace—places where sellers list their property for sale by owner. I contact the owners and negotiate owner financing. I've also financed a project where a property owner allowed me to build a home on his property. When the home was sold, I paid the property owner their asking price for the land. You can also check with a realtor and have them look through the MLS to see if any of the properties listed for sale offer seller financing.

Novations

A novation is one of those strategies not everyone knows about, but it can be a game changer in real estate investing when used right. So, what's a novation? You may have seen it in action without realizing it on the HGTV show *Unsellable Homes*. In simple terms, it's when you, as the investor, step in to help the seller by taking over the deal and bringing in a new buyer to close it. You're essentially acting as a middleman, and you're not actually buying the property yourself. You're just facilitating the sale.

Here's how it works:

1. **Agreement with the Seller**: You and the seller sign a contract where they agree to let you take control of marketing and selling their property. They give you the authority to negotiate with buyers on their behalf.
2. **Find a Buyer**: You bring in a new buyer. Often this is someone who can pay more than what you agreed to pay the seller.
3. **Close the Deal**: When the deal closes, the seller gets the amount you agreed on, and you keep the difference as your profit. Everyone walks away happy.

Now, why would a seller go for this? Well, maybe their property needs work, or they're in a tough spot and don't have the resources to get it sold on their own. You're stepping in to handle the process for them, which saves them time and hassle. It's a win-win.

Let me give you an example. Say a seller has a property they want $200,000 for, but it's worth $250,000 on the open market after some minor updates. You step in, agree to pay them $200,000, and then market the property to a buyer for $250,000. When the sale closes, the seller gets their $200,000, and you pocket the $50,000 difference. This pays off the investment you made to do the small updates, while the rest is profit.

The great thing about novations is that you're not using your own money to buy the property. Instead, you're leveraging your skills, network, and resources to add value and make the deal happen. It's a low-risk, high-reward strategy if you do it right. Of course, like anything in real estate, you've got to have the right paperwork in place. A solid novation agreement is key, and I'd always recommend working with a good attorney to ensure everything is above board.

What I love about novations is they're all about creating opportunities where others might see obstacles. It's about being resourceful, solving problems, and helping everyone involved walk away with a win. And that's the Pono Way!

LEVERAGING EXISTING INVESTMENTS

There are a few other ways to get creative when funding your real estate deals that don't involve sellers.

Whole Life Insurance Policies

One creative strategy I've seen people use to fund real estate deals—and I've used it myself—is to leverage a whole life insurance policy. It's one of those things a lot of folks don't even think about, but it can be a powerful tool when you use it right.

With a whole life policy, you're not just paying for insurance. You're also building up cash value over time. That cash value is like a savings account inside your policy. The cool part is you can borrow against it. So, if you've been paying into your policy for years and have built up enough cash value, you can tap into that money and use it to fund your next real estate deal.

Let's say you're looking at a property and need some quick capital for the down payment or to cover renovations.

Instead of pulling money out of your savings or scrambling for a loan, you can take out a loan from your own policy. And get this—it's not like borrowing from a bank where you're begging for approval or dealing with strict terms. You're essentially borrowing from yourself, and you set the repayment terms.

The best part? While you're using that loan for your real estate deal, the cash value in your policy keeps growing as if you never took the money out. That's because the loan is secured against the policy, not the cash value itself. So, your money works double-time by funding your deal and earning returns in the policy.

Now, there are a few things to keep in mind. First, you'll need to pay back the loan with interest, but here's the kicker—you're paying the interest back to your own policy. It's like paying yourself instead of a bank. Second, you need to be disciplined about repayment. If you don't pay it back, it could reduce your policy's death benefit or create issues down the line.

Using a whole life policy this way is all about having options. It gives you flexibility and access to capital without tapping into traditional financing or risking other investments. For me, it's all about thinking outside the box. If you've got a policy and a real estate opportunity, this might be the perfect combo to make it happen. Before you act, make sure to consult with your insurance agent and financial advisor to ensure this is a good option for you.

Self-Directed 401(k)

You could use your 401(k), especially if it's self-directed through a broker. A self-directed 401(k) gives you more control over how your retirement funds are invested, including the ability to use those funds for real estate deals. You'll want to work with a knowledgeable broker to make sure everything is set up properly, but this can be a powerful—and tax-saving—tool for funding your investments without dipping into your savings.

Stocks

And let's not forget about stocks. If you or someone in your network has investments in the stock market, they could liquidate some of those assets to fund your deal. It's rare that a person could get as good a return on investment playing the stock market as they can with real estate! Maybe it's your own portfolio, or maybe you've got a partner or private lender who's willing to cash out some of their stocks to invest in your project. Stocks can be a quick source of capital when the timing is right. Just make sure you're aware of any taxes you'll be required to pay on money from liquidated stocks.

IMPORTANT THINGS TO REMEMBER ABOUT FUNDING

The key is to be ready to move fast. When you start working to lock up a deal, you're not the only investor looking at it—others are ready to jump in if you don't act quickly. That's why cash offers are so appealing to sellers. They don't have to wait through the longer process it takes to secure a conventional loan, which makes your offer even more attractive.

Most purchase contracts include a financing contingency, which allows you, as the buyer, to back out of the deal if you can't secure financing. Sellers know this, which is why they often prefer to work with investors who can move faster and don't need that contingency in the contract.

Once your offer is accepted, you'll need to put down an earnest money deposit (EMD) to show you're serious about the deal. This amount can range from $1,000 to $10,000 or more, depending on the property and what you've agreed upon. The EMD helps reassure the seller that you're committed to moving forward.

From there, the process moves into escrow (more on that in the next section). This is the time to finalize your funding. Whether you're using a bank, private money, or hard money, you'll need everything lined up before closing. This is also when the inspection period comes into play—which usually lasts around 14 days. During this time, you can inspect the property and make sure everything checks out, while also securing the funds needed to close the deal.

Now, I'll be honest—this part can be stressful. As investors, we don't always have the full amount ready when the offer is accepted, so we're often working hard during those 14 days to lock down private money lenders or other funding sources. And just to clear up a common misconception: When we talk about making a "cash offer," it doesn't mean you're showing up at the escrow office with a briefcase full of cash. The payment is made through certified funds, like a cashier's check or wire transfer, which goes directly through the banks. That's how the seller gets paid—it's all handled securely and professionally.

The key here, during this stressful time, is flexibility. Real estate investing isn't always about having cash in hand—it's about knowing how to unlock the resources you already have or finding people who can bring resources to the table with them. Whether it's equity, retirement funds, or stock investments, there are plenty of ways to leverage what you've got to create opportunities to get the money you need to make a deal happen. Once you start thinking outside the box, you'll see there are so many ways to fund your deals. That's how you grow and scale as an investor.

MAIN TAKEAWAYS FROM CHAPTER 7.7

1. **I've said it before, and I'll say it again. You don't need your own money to fund a deal.** One of the biggest myths in real estate is thinking you need to have cash in the bank to get started. I didn't. Most of my students don't, either. The truth is, you can use other people's money—through hard money lenders, private investors, or creative financing—to fund your deals.

2. **Private money is all about relationships and trust.** You don't have to go to a bank to get funding. Sometimes the best funding comes from people you already know—friends, family, or community members who want a better return on their money. When they trust you and your plan, they're more likely to say yes.

3. **The best funding deals are built on win-wins.** Whether you're using a private lender, a hard money loan, or creative financing, make sure everyone benefits. You get to do the deal, and your lender gets a solid return. That's the kind of partnership that leads to long-term success.

4. **You've got to present your deals with confidence.** No one will hand over money if you're unsure about your numbers or your plan. Show up prepared. Know your deal inside and out. When you speak with clarity and confidence, people will believe in you—and they'll invest.

Chapter 7.8

Closing the Deal

The escrow process is a critical step in closing any real estate deal. In Hawaii, there are some specific steps and requirements to the escrow process that are different from other places. In this section of the chapter, I'm going to break those down for you, so you know exactly what to do during escrow. Later in this section, I'm also going to cover the next—and my favorite—step in the real estate investing process: project management.

The process of escrow acts like the middleman who ensures everything goes smoothly between you and the seller. In Hawaii, you must have an escrow company manage this process. The escrow company acts as a neutral third party that protects both parties and ensures the deal is handled correctly. But before you go into escrow, you'll first need a purchase contract.

THE PURCHASE CONTRACT

The purchase contract is a legally binding agreement between you (the investor) and the seller. It's a crucial part of any real estate deal because it spells out the details of the deal, like the price and timelines. Plus, it lays out any contingencies that need to be met before the property changes hands. This document details all the terms and conditions you and the seller have agreed on, making sure everyone's on the same page. Think of it as the roadmap for getting the deal done.

The key elements you'll usually find in a purchase contract include:

1. **Buyer and Seller Info**: Your name, the seller's name, plus contact details
2. **Property Details**: The address and legal description of the property you're buying
3. **Purchase Price**: How much you're paying for the property
4. **Earnest Money Deposit (EMD)**: The amount of money you're putting down to show you're serious about the deal
5. **Contingencies**: Conditions that must be met before the sale is finalized, like financing approval, inspection results, or appraisals
6. **Inspection Period**: The timeline for inspections, often called the J-1 period in Hawaii
7. **Closing Date**: When you'll officially take ownership of the property
8. **Special Terms or Addendums**: Any additional agreements, like repairs the seller agrees to make or items included in the sale (appliances, furniture, etc.)

The purchase contract protects both you and the seller because it makes sure all the terms of the deal are clear, so there's no confusion about who's responsible for what. Once the purchase contract is signed, the seller can't back out of the deal without facing legal consequences. Plus it gives you, the investor, an "out" if something goes wrong during the inspection or financing process. For example, if the property has termite damage or unpermitted work, the purchase contract might allow you to renegotiate the price or back out without losing your EMD.

Where can you get a purchase contract? Usually, your real estate agent will prepare one for you using standard forms specific to your state or region. If you're working on an off-market deal without an agent, you can use a template. I always recommend having an attorney—familiar with real estate and the escrow process in Hawaii—review the purchase contract to make sure it's solid. We make Hawaii-specific purchase contracts available to HUI Academy and Mastermind members to save them the work and expense of creating their own, which is just one of the many benefits of working with us.

OPENING ESCROW

Two things are required to open escrow. First, you and the seller must agree on the terms of the deal and sign a purchase contract. Second, you must make an earnest money deposit to the escrow company. The EMD shows you're serious about the deal. The amount can vary, depending on the property and how committed you want to appear to the seller. With a traditional purchase (meaning it isn't a wholesale deal), the EMD will typically be 1%–3% of the purchase price.

With wholesale deals, the EMD is often lower to minimize risk. Once the escrow company receives the EMD, escrow officially opens.

The escrow company holds the EMD and ensures all paperwork, payments, and inspections are handled properly. They will also work with the seller and investor to ensure the title is clean and there are no legal issues with the property.

The J-1 Inspection Period

Once escrow is open, the J-1 inspection period begins. This lasts anywhere from 7 to 14 days, and it's one of the most important parts of your real estate deal because it gives you a chance to mobilize your Dream Team and start doing your homework on the property. This is when you'll want to bring in contractors, home inspectors, and even specialists to check for code violations, unpermitted areas, structural issues like foundation or roof problems, and open permits.

During the J-1 inspection period, you can renegotiate the purchase price or even back out of the deal if something big comes up—all without losing your EMD. But you can't just walk away for any reason. It must be valid and tied to the inspection. Here are some legit reasons to back out:

- **Structural Issues.** If the property has major structural problems, like a cracked foundation, sinking floors, or serious roof damage, that's a big red flag. Fixing those kinds of issues can cost a fortune, and unless the seller is willing to renegotiate the price, it might be smarter to walk away.
- **Unpermitted Work.** If the inspection reveals unpermitted additions or renovations, you could be

looking at fines, code violations, or costly fixes to bring the property up to code. This is a valid reason to back out, especially if the seller wasn't upfront about it.

- **Termite or Pest Damage.** In Hawaii, termites are a real problem. Severe infestations can cause significant structural damage. If the termite inspection shows major damage, you can back out unless the seller agrees to cover the repairs.

- **Plumbing, Electrical, or HVAC Problems.** If the systems that make the home livable—like plumbing, electrical, or heating and cooling—are in bad shape, that's another reason to reconsider. These are critical systems and fixing them could really break your renovations budget.

- **Title Issues.** Title problems aren't directly tied to the physical inspection, but they can still cause expensive legal issues that could make the property a bad investment for you. If a title search reveals liens, disputes, or other legal issues with the property, these could all be reasons to back out of the deal. You can have a real estate attorney search for title issues, or you can do it yourself by visiting Hawaii's Bureau of Conveyances website and using the Land Title Records Search to look up the property by its Tax Map Key or the owner's name.

- **Environmental Hazards.** Hawaii is a beautiful place like no other, but the beauty can come with a price. Properties in lava zones or flood zones can be risky investments. If you discover the property is in a high-risk area or has environmental issues like soil contamination or asbestos, you may want to back out and look for a better deal. I'll talk more about this in chapter 9.

- **Appraisal Gaps.** If the appraisal comes back lower than what you and the seller agreed on, and the seller isn't willing to adjust the price, you could use this as a valid reason to back out of the deal.
- **Survey or Setback Issues.** Are there boundary disputes or setback intrusions? Those can be red flags, too. Issues like these can be expensive to resolve and might limit how you can use the property.
- **Cost of Repairs.** Sometimes a contractor estimate can make all the difference. If the estimated cost of repairs or renovations is way higher than you expected, that could affect the deal's profitability and be a deal breaker for you. If you want to back out due to high repair costs, make sure you have documentation to support your claim, like the home inspection report, a detailed contractor estimate for repairs or renovations, and any findings you have from structural engineers or termite inspectors. These documents help prove there are legitimate issues, not just buyer's remorse.
- **Personal Financing Issues.** If you can't secure financing due to unexpected reasons during the inspection period, you may be able to back out without penalty.

That's a pretty long list, right? But it's important to know what is on it because you want to protect yourself if any of these issues come up. To be certain you can back out of a deal if you need to, here are my hard and fast rules for the J-1 inspection period.

First, document everything. ALWAYS get everything in writing.

Second, get a detailed report of the home inspection from a licensed home inspector.

Third, work closely with the real estate agent to make sure all contingencies are clear in the contract. The inspection period is also where having a good real estate agent and doing your due diligence pays off. Verify the property details, like the number of bedrooms and bathrooms, by checking tax records and planning department documents. Trust me, you don't want to end up buying a "three-bedroom" house that's only legally a "one-bedroom," like I mentioned earlier. Just ask my business partner, Zasha. That's not fun.

I also recommend doing a final walk-through of the property with your contractor to check for any issues. That final walk-through is your last chance to get out of the deal without losing your EMD. Sometimes the J-1 inspection period isn't long enough for you to accomplish due diligence or secure financing. When that happens, you can request an extension, as long as the seller also agrees to the extension terms.

If you're wholesaling, the J-1 inspection period is also when you can assign the contract to another buyer. Just ensure all parties are aware and agree to the assignment terms. Assignment terms are the rules for how you pass your purchase contract on to someone else. So, let's say you've got a property under contract during your J-1 inspection period, but instead of buying it yourself, you find another buyer who wants it. You can assign your rights in that contract to them—for a fee, of course.

Everyone involved—the seller, the end buyer, and you—needs to be clear and in agreement about that arrangement. It's not something you do behind the scenes. You want to make sure the paperwork spells it all out—what you're selling the contract for, how you're getting paid, and when the new buyer steps in. That way, nobody's surprised, and you stay on the right side of things.

THE CLOSING PROCESS

Let's say you've walked through the entire J-1 inspection period. Everything has checked out, and you're ready to proceed to closing. Here's what you'll need before closing can take place.

First up, you'll need homeowners insurance that includes coverage for flood and hurricane damage. If you're financing the property with a traditional lender, they'll require it and may have suggestions for insurance agents or companies you can use. If you're paying with cash or using private money, it's on you to find an insurance agent. You can also ask local real estate agents which insurance agents they trust.

You'll also need to secure funding. As you near the closing date—usually 30 to 45 days after escrow opens—you'll need the remaining funds to complete the purchase. Hawaii has a Good Funds Law that requires all funds to clear before closing can happen. This means you'll probably need to sign additional funding acknowledgments confirming the escrow company received the money in time.

Once financing is secured, the money gets wired from the lender or lenders. If it's a cash purchase, a cashier's check will be sent straight to the escrow company. For mainland buyers, wire transfers are the norm, so be aware of time zone differences to avoid delays. The escrow company handles all transfers, pays the seller, and ensures everything is legally binding.

I would say closing a real estate deal is like crossing a finish line. You've put in a lot of hard work, and you can see how it's all going to pay off…but there's a stack of paperwork to sign before you can grab those keys. So, let me walk you through the most important documents you'll come across during the closing process.

Closing Disclosure (CD): If you're using financing, this document lays out all the final terms of your loan, including the loan amount, interest rate, monthly payments, and closing costs. Plus, it describes who's paying them. You'll get the CD a few days before closing. Review it carefully to make sure everything matches what you were promised.

Deed: The deed is the legal document that transfers ownership of the property from the seller to you. The deed will include the property's legal description and your name as the new owner.

Settlement Statement (HUD-1 or ALTA): This document itemizes all financial aspects of the transaction, including purchase price, EMD, loan amount, prorated property taxes and estimated utilities—plus other fees or adjustments. This statement ensures all the money is accounted for and shows what you and the seller owe at closing.

Promissory Note: If you're taking out a loan, you'll also need to sign a promissory note. This is basically the IOU for your mortgage and includes the loan amount, repayment terms, interest rate information, and default consequences if you can't keep up with the payments.

Mortgage: This document secures the loan using the property as collateral, which gives the lender the right to foreclose if you don't meet your loan obligations.

Bill of Sale: Sometimes the property owner agrees to include personal property in the sale, like appliances or furniture. A Bill of Sale transfers ownership of any personal property to the investor. If you negotiated for the seller to leave anything behind, make sure it's listed here.

Hawaii-Specific Title Insurance Policy: Title insurance is common everywhere and protects you and your lender against title defects, like liens or disputes over ownership. Hawaii's title insurance policies, however, may also include exceptions or addendums for unique local issues, like shoreline boundaries or Hawaiian cultural sites. You'll review and sign documents acknowledging these specifics.

Affidavits and Declarations: You'll sign affidavits confirming you're not purchasing the property under false pretenses and that any issues found during title searches have been resolved.

Insurance Acknowledgment: If you're financing the deal, lenders usually require proof of homeowners insurance. You'll sign a document confirming coverage is in place.

Leasehold or Fee Simple Documents: Hawaii has leasehold properties, where the land is leased rather than owned outright. If you're buying a leasehold property, additional documents related to the lease agreement, landowner terms, and lease expiration will need to be signed. If it's fee simple (you own the land outright), this won't apply.

Lease Agreements (if applicable): If the property has tenants or you're buying it as a rental, you'll sign documents acknowledging the transfer of any leases.

Lien Waivers (if applicable): If the property had work done before closing, you may need signed lien waivers from contractors to ensure they don't place liens on the property after you take ownership.

Tax Documents: If the seller is not a Hawaii resident, the Hawaii Real Property Tax Act (HARPTA) requires that 7.25% of the sales price be withheld for taxes. Documents related to HARPTA withholding are unique to Hawaii and must be signed during closing. This ensures compliance with state tax laws. If the seller is a foreign national, Hawaii also adheres to the Foreign Investment in Real Property Tax Act (FIRPTA) federal tax withholding, which may require additional documents for both buyer and seller to sign. You'll also sign W-9 forms and other tax-related documents that report the purchase to the IRS.

Survey and Termite Inspection Acknowledgments: In Hawaii, properties often require you to sign survey acknowledgment documents that confirm the property boundaries and that there are no encroachments or setback violations. And since termites are common in Hawaii, both the buyer and seller may also need to acknowledge and address any termite findings before closing by signing a termite inspection report.

Lava Zone and Natural Hazard Disclosures: Hawaii has unique risks, like lava zones and tsunami evacuation areas. (I'll go into more detail later in the book.) You'll likely sign Natural Hazard Disclosures, confirming that you understand the property's location-related risks. This is especially important on the Big Island, where lava zones can affect insurance and financing.

If this seems like a lot of documents, it is! Here's my best advice for making all the paperwork more manageable. Ask for copies of the documents a few days before closing. This will give you a chance to review everything ahead of time, so you're not rushed on the day of closing. Don't forget to bring a government-issued photo ID with you to finalize the deal. And don't hesitate to ask questions about anything you don't understand. This is your investment, and it pays to be thorough.

After all the documents are signed, they must be recorded with the Bureau of Conveyances in Honolulu before the transfer of ownership is official. This can take a few days, so possession isn't immediate after signing like it is in other states. Once the paperwork is all recorded, the deal is considered closed, and you'll get refunded any surplus from the transaction. Then you'll get the keys to your new property, and you'll have a big smile on your face because— in my opinion—the fun is just getting started.

MAIN TAKEAWAYS FROM CHAPTER 7.8

1. **Closing the deal is where everything becomes real.** This is the finish line of all your hard work—where the paperwork gets signed and ownership officially transfers. But don't relax just yet. You've got to stay locked in and follow the tips in the chapter to ensure every detail is handled the right way.

2. **Communication with your title company or escrow officer is key.** These are the folks making sure the deal closes clean. You need to be in regular contact, double-check documents, and respond quickly if something comes up. A smooth close depends on good communication and follow-through.

3. **Don't forget your due diligence—right up to the end.** Before you close, make sure you've handled inspections, verified funding, reviewed final numbers, and checked that the title is clear. Rushing through this part can cost you big time later. Make sure to finish strong.

4. **Celebrate—but also get ready for the next phase.** Once you close, the real work begins—whether that's a renovation, a resale, or setting up tenants. Take a moment to celebrate, then shift gears and stay focused on the next step in your investing journey.

Chapter 7.9

Managing the Project

Congratulations! You've successfully closed your first (or next) deal. Now my favorite part of real estate investing can begin—managing the project. The property is finally yours, and it's time to get it whipped into shape so you can sell or rent it. This is where the rubber meets the road, and hiring the right contractor is absolutely critical. You may already have one on your Dream Team by now, but if you're still looking, remember you need someone who's licensed, insured, and reliable.

WORKING WITH CONTRACTORS

A good, licensed contractor is worth their weight in gold when it comes to your real estate investing projects. The best way to find good contractors is through referrals. Talk to other investors or homeowners who have worked with them personally, and read their reviews. You can also find contractors when you're out driving around and see crews working on houses. Don't hesitate to check out their projects and get their contact info.

When you do choose a contractor, here are some of my best tips for working with them.

First, contracts are a MUST

I said it before, and I'll say it again—you need *everything* in writing, so there's no question about who's responsible for what. This includes the timeline, the roles of the contractor and their team, and the way to settle issues if there's a dispute. A solid contract is your best friend if things go sideways. Not sure where to find or how to create a contract like this? Here are some places you can look:

- **Real Estate Attorneys** I think your best bet, at least in the beginning, is to hire a real estate attorney to draft a custom contract. That way you can tailor the contract to your specific project in a way that protects your interests and complies with local laws. A real estate attorney can spot any red flags in the contractor's terms. You're investing time and money in this renovation, so it's worth doing it right. While this costs more upfront, it can save you a ton of headaches if disputes arise.
- **The Contractor Themselves** Many licensed general contractors will have their own standard contracts. These can be a good starting point, but don't just sign them without reading carefully. Contractors' contracts are often written to protect them more than you, so it's a smart move to review them thoroughly—and have your lawyer go over them—to ensure your interests are also covered.
- **State or Local Building Departments** In some states or counties, building departments offer templates for

construction contracts that meet local regulations. While Hawaii doesn't have a statewide standard contract, check your local building department or look online at official county websites.

- **Online Contract Templates** There are plenty of websites where you can download or purchase construction contract templates designed for real estate projects, including the American Institute of Architects, LegalZoom or Rocket Lawyer, and construction-specific sites like Levelset or Construction Contract Writer.
- **Investor Networks or Mentorship Programs** If you're part of a real estate investment group or mentorship program, ask around. Experienced investors often have contractor contracts they've used and are willing to share. You might even get a sample contract that's already been tested in the field. This is something we offer our HUI Academy and Mastermind members.
- **DIY (with Guidance)** If you have a legal background or are comfortable drafting your own contract, you could start with a basic template and tweak it for your needs. Make sure you have a lawyer review the contract before using it, though.

No matter how you choose to create the contract, ensure it includes the information I'm listing below, and have an attorney or experienced investor review it to make sure it's solid. A good project contract needs to include:

Scope of Work: Always have a scope of work that outlines the entire project. This includes start and end dates, demo phases, renovation tasks, framing, concrete work, and more. It keeps everyone on the same page and helps avoid misunderstandings. You can even include information about:

- Whether or not you'll charge penalties for delays and how much those penalties will be
- How you will handle change orders and added work
- Dispute resolution guidelines that outline what happens if you and the contractor don't agree

Lien Waivers: Here's another thing many rookie investors overlook—lien waivers. Make it a standard part of your process to have every contractor and subcontractor sign a lien waiver when they get paid. If they don't sign a lien waiver, and they claim later that they weren't paid, they can slap a lien on your property. That'll mess up your title, slow down your project, and can even kill a sale if you're trying to flip. I've seen deals fall apart over this. It doesn't matter if you *did* pay them—without that signed waiver, it's your word against theirs. So, keep those lien waivers on file for every draw or payment. It's a simple habit that protects your project and your profits.

Payment Schedule: Never pay a contractor upfront. Instead, include a payment schedule tied to project phases in the contract. For example, pay after the demo is done, after framing is completed, and so on. A payment schedule helps ensure that work gets done before the money is handed over.

Think about it like this: When you get hired at McDonald's, they don't pay you upfront—you work for two weeks before you get your first paycheck. The same principle applies here.

You may even want to consider retainage, which means holding back a portion of each payment until the project is completed to your specifications.

As the project progresses, be prepared to do regular inspections throughout the renovation. Many hard money lenders will require these inspections to release construction draws. It's also a good way to stay aligned with the contractor on progress.

MANAGING PROJECTS YOURSELF

But what if you're planning to manage your own project without hiring a licensed general contractor? Managing your own project can help save you money and help you maintain more control over the project, but there are certain rules and restrictions around owner-builder projects specific to the state of Hawaii you will need to abide by. The main one is called the owner-builder law.

The Owner-Builder Law

In Hawaii, the owner-builder law applies mainly to folks building or improving properties for personal use, not flipping or renting. The big rule is this: If you take out an owner-builder permit, you can't sell or lease the property for at least one year after it's completed and passed final inspection.[1] This is to keep people from skirting the licensing system and flipping properties without proper oversight.

If you have an owner-builder permit, that means you're responsible for a bunch of things that a licensed general contractor would otherwise take care of for you, like:

- Getting all necessary building permits
- Complying with local building codes and making sure everything passes inspection
- Overseeing all the work and hiring subcontractors who are licensed and insured
- Liability. If something goes wrong—say, the structure doesn't meet code or there's an accident—it's on you
- Keeping records of all work, including contracts, receipts, and permits for at least three years

Now, if something unexpected comes up—like a health issue or relocation—you can apply for a hardship exemption through the Contractors License Board. They might give you permission to sell or lease earlier, but you'll need a solid reason. You can learn more about these regulations from Hawaii's Department of Commerce and Consumer Affairs (DCCA).[2]

County-Specific Considerations

In addition to the state laws, each county in Hawaii has its own building codes, zoning rules, and permit requirements. For example, some counties might have stricter timelines or rules for inspections, or zoning laws that could affect what you're allowed to build or renovate. Before you dive into a project, make sure you check with the local building department in the county where the property is located. Whether you're on Oahu, Maui, Kauai, or the Big Island, each county office will help you understand any extra hoops you may need to jump through.

What Happens If You Don't Follow the Rules?

If you violate the owner-builder laws, the penalties aren't light. For a first offense, you could be looking at a fine of up to $5,000 or 50% of the permit value, whichever is higher. If it happens again, the fines get steeper, and you could lose the ability to apply for owner-builder permits for three years. Trust me, you don't want to mess with this. Here's my best advice for making sure your project management goes off without a hitch.

1. **First, check with the county.** Always start by talking to the local building department. They'll fill you in on any county-specific rules that could impact your project.

2. **Think ahead.** If there's a chance you'll need to sell or lease the property within a year, it might be smarter to hire a licensed general contractor to avoid the owner-builder restriction.

3. **Keep good records at every stage of the project.** I know I said it earlier, but get everything in writing! Stay on top of your paperwork, including permits, contracts, and invoices, so you're covered if anyone starts asking questions.

Owner-builder projects can be a great way to take control of your investment and save money, but you've got to play by the rules. Do your homework, and you'll save yourself a lot of headaches down the road.

BUDGET TRACKING AND TAXES

Speaking of money, let's talk about the financials when it comes to managing projects. I'm not a financial or tax advisor, and this should not be considered financial or tax advice. Make sure you talk to your financial advisor and tax expert to create a plan that aligns with your goals. Here's what works for me when it comes to managing a project's budget.

I recommend opening a separate checking account for each project. This way, you can clearly see what's being spent on materials, labor, and other expenses. I also like to use a spreadsheet to track everything. Having all your info in one place will save you headaches later.

As an investor, you'll also need to 1099 your contractors, so you're not stuck paying taxes on money you're paying out. Make sure your contractors provide a W-9 form and keep everything documented.

IMPORTANT DOCUMENTS

Here's a checklist of documents I recommend for every project:

- Contract with the contractor
  - » Scope of work
  - » Payment schedule
- W-9 form
- Hold harmless agreement (a legal document where one party agrees not to hold the other party responsible if something goes wrong)
- Lien waiver (to protect you from unpaid subcontractors placing a lien on the property)

FINAL STEPS

Once the renovation is done, do a final walk-through with the contractor and complete a punch list. A punch list is a comprehensive list of everything that was supposed to be done. You'll walk through the property and check things off, noting any unfinished or minor corrections that need to be wrapped up. Managing a project the right way isn't only about fixing up a house—it's about protecting your investment and setting yourself up for success.

CONGRATULATIONS! When renovations and repairs are completed, you're ready to decide whether you want to sell or rent the property. You're also ready to start thinking about finding your next deal and the next.

If you need a refresher on how to locate your next deal, head back to section 7.4.

You've probably noticed me talking about what a unique market Hawaii real estate is. There are a number of factors that play into that, including our history and culture, as well as the land itself. In part 3 of this book, I'm going to share the blessings and challenges of Hawaii real estate investing. This will be especially helpful for mainlanders who aren't as familiar with Hawaii and the Hawaii real estate market. Plus, it's a great refresher for any locals interested in investing, even if you've lived here your whole life.

Then as I bring this book to a close, in part 4, I'll send you off with a step-by-step Business Blueprint to help you get ready to invest in Hawaii real estate. You're going to love this because it really sets you up for success from the very beginning, and I'm including a lot of resources and bonus content that normally only HUI Academy and Mastermind students get.

Aloha!

MAIN TAKEAWAYS FROM CHAPTER 7.9

1. **There are two ways to manage projects—do it yourself or hire a project manager.** There's no right or wrong answer. Choose the route that matches your skill level, budget, and schedule.

2. **If you're hiring a project manager, make sure you have a good contract.** Get everything in writing before the first hammer swings, including scope of work, materials list, budget, and timeline.

3. **If you're managing projects yourself, make sure you're familiar with the rules and restrictions around owner-builder projects in Hawaii.** If you violate the owner-builder laws, the penalties aren't light.

4. **Work with contractors you trust and treat them right.** Your contractor is one of the most important people on your team. Vet them carefully, communicate clearly, and pay them on time. When you build mutual respect, they'll take care of your projects like their own.

PART 3

Blessings and Challenges in Paradise

Chapter 8

Brief History of the Land

Hawaii's history is a huge part of what makes our real estate market on the islands so unique. The way land has been used and owned here is deeply tied to our culture, traditions, and even some hard lessons from the past. If you want to invest in Hawaii real estate—especially if you live on the mainland or aren't a native Hawaiian—you've got to understand where it all started. Hawaii's history impacts the way we do things the Pono Way today in real estate.

Hawaii became a state on August 21, 1959, making it the 50th state of the United States. It's the only state made up entirely of islands and the only one located in the Pacific Ocean. Statehood isn't even close to the beginning of the story, though. Hawaii was a US territory first, after being annexed by the United States in 1898. And before that...well, the islands have always been here, inhabited for centuries by a people rich in culture. Let's start there, with the story of the Hawaiian people.

The history I'm about to tell you is current and correct to the best of my knowledge, but I'm not perfect. I want to retell the story of Hawaiian history as it truly was, but please correct me if I'm wrong.

THE AHUPUA'A SYSTEM

One of my favorite parts of Hawaiian history is the *ahupua'a* system. This ancient land management method was smart because it was deeply rooted in respect for the 'āina (land). People were serious about stewarding the land and taking care of it. The principles of the ahupua'a system continue to influence how Hawaiians approach real estate and land stewardship.

What was the ahupua'a system?

Back in ancient Hawaii, the land was divided into sections called ahupua'a, which stretched from the *mauka* (mountains) all the way to the *makai* (ocean). If you hear Hawaiians talking about "from the mountains to the sea," the ahupua'a system is what we're talking about. Each ahupua'a contained a variety of ecosystems, providing each community with all the resources they needed.

For example, each ahupua'a had forests and mountains for timber and wild game, streams for fresh water, agricultural land for farming taro and sweet potatoes, and ocean areas for fishing and salt gathering. Many sections also had *heiau* (temples) that helped keep the spiritual connection between the land and its people strong. Because every ahupua'a had everything it needed, the communities inside could be self-sufficient and live off the land. The system was overseen by *ali'i* (chiefs) and *konohiki* (land managers) who made sure that the land was used wisely and that everyone cared for it.[1]

How has the ahupuaʻa system positively influenced Hawaii real estate?

Although the ahupuaʻa system is no longer used officially, its values are carried forward with a modern-day focus on sustainability, stewardship, and proper zoning—all principles that mesh with doing real estate investing the Pono Way.

When it comes to sustainability, we want to live in harmony with the land. As a real estate developer, I look for ways to be eco-friendly so our beautiful islands will be preserved for future generations, a principle I also teach to my HUI Academy and Mastermind students.

As more and more Hawaiians leave the islands, there are fewer of us here to pass on our culture and traditions. We need more real estate investors who care about landowners and who get to know them as people to create deals that are a win for everyone. These investors can become stewards of our culture by making it affordable for native Hawaiians to live here.

Zoning in Hawaii is really unique. In many ways, modern zoning laws still support ahupuaʻa divisions and respect natural boundaries. If land was agricultural during ahupuaʻa times, it's likely still zoned as agricultural today.[2]

What current challenges are rooted in the ahupuaʻa system?

The ahupuaʻa system's legacy has created a few unique challenges for Hawaii real estate investors. Being familiar with these challenges and understanding how to best deal with them is important, and while I want to give you an overview here, I'll cover each one in more detail in the next chapter.

The first challenge is access issues. Some properties follow ancient land divisions, which can make it hard to get to a piece of land if it's surrounded by private property with no access. Understanding these historical divisions is crucial for modern land transactions.

The second challenge is conservation land. Many former ahupuaʻa areas are now designated as conservation lands. This can limit what you can and can't do on a piece of property when it is designated this way. There are also certain species—like sea turtles and monk seals—that are protected, and that requires careful planning to navigate sometimes.

The third challenge you need to be aware of that stems from ahupuaʻa times are the cultural sites and historical landmarks. There are many protected areas that are important to our culture, and some include burial sites. It's not uncommon for developers to unearth human bones in the more rural areas during construction, yet this can be an issue even in urban areas. Over the years, developers have unintentionally unearthed the remains of more than 200 people during different construction projects in Waikiki. To honor and show respect for the dead, a burial mound for those remains called Kahi Haliʻa Aloha (the place of cherished memories) was built.

THE GREAT MĀHELE

In the late 1700s and early 1800s, Western explorers, missionaries, and traders arrived in Hawaii and brought new ideas about property ownership, government, and economics—all systems geared more toward profit instead of stewardship. As these influences started to take effect, the ahupua'a system gradually fell out of use. The final nail in the coffin for the ahupua'a system happened when King Kamehameha III signed the Great Māhele into effect in 1848, dividing Hawaiian land into private property.

Before that, land wasn't owned in the Western sense—it was communal. The *ali'i* (chiefs) and *konohiki* (land managers) oversaw it, and the people who lived on it had rights to use it. No one "owned" it outright. The Māhele changed that by breaking up the land into private property.

The Great Māhele gave land to the monarchy, government, and chiefs allowing private ownership of land for the first time. About 23% of the land was considered The King's Lands, reserved for Kamehameha III and the monarchy. The government got 37% of the land for public use, and the chiefs and land managers got about 39%. That left just 1% of the land for common people. These parcels of land are called kuleana lands. They can't be deeded and can only be granted to Native Hawaiians. Many Native Hawaiians lost their land over time because they didn't understand the laws or couldn't pay taxes on the land they were given.

The Great Māhele had another major impact on Hawaiians. In 1950, foreigners, who weren't allowed to own land before, gained the right to buy property. Large tracts of land were sold or leased to sugar and pineapple plantation owners, ushering in the plantation economy. Instead of communal land that was self-sufficient and sustainable under the ahupuaʻa system, plantations were geared toward farming a single crop for profit. Hawaiian land ended up in the hands of a few families or companies, which still shapes the real estate market in Hawaii today.

How does the Great Māhele impact real estate investing today?

Many large tracts of land are still controlled by a handful of trusts and estates that trace their ownership back to the Māhele. Examples include the Bishop Estate (Kamehameha Schools), the Robinson family on Kauai, and the Parker Ranch on the Big Island. As an investor, you might find yourself negotiating with these entities, which often have strict guidelines for how their land is used. When dealing with any of these organizations, you'll really have to do your homework to understand the historical context of the property to invest well.

The Great Māhele also affected who owned which lands. If you look at the most beautiful beaches in Hawaii, you'll notice a pattern when it comes to who owns that land. For the most part, the most beautiful areas on the islands are owned by United States government military bases. Under the Bishop Trust (one of the richest trusts in the world), these lands are leased to the United States government for a dollar, while Native Hawaiians struggle to afford to live in their own homeland.

When land ownership laws changed, leasehold properties became common in Hawaii. With a leasehold, you don't own the land outright. Instead, you lease it from a landowner or trust, like the Bishop Trust, for a set period, often between

50 and 99 years. This is a direct result of the large estates holding onto land while allowing others to use it. Leasehold properties can be good investments, but you need to understand the terms and expiration of the lease. Here's the thing—even if you "purchase" property located on Bishop lands, you don't actually own the land. You can only buy the home and rent the land, and the land will return to the trust after a certain number of years.

A KINGDOM OVERTHROWN

Things changed again in 1893, when Queen Liliʻuokalani, the last monarch of Hawaii, was overthrown. A group of American and European businessmen, backed by the US military, orchestrated a coup so they could control more of Hawaii's land and resources and avoid tariffs on sugar exports to the US, which hurt their profits. Hawaii was annexed in 1898 and became an American territory.

How does Hawaii's annexation impact real estate investing today?

Annexation put Hawaii under American law, which opened the door to foreign investment and development. Much of Hawaii's land ended up owned by large companies or wealthy families. Because of this, the amount of land available for private ownership is limited. Property is in high demand from locals, mainland buyers, and international investors, causing Hawaii to have some of the highest property prices in the US.

Annexation also introduced fee simple ownership to Hawaii, meaning that for the first time, land could be bought, sold, or transferred freely. It also ushered in the start of leasehold properties, where buyers own the building but lease the land. This system is still common today, especially in areas with historical ties to plantations or large estates.

When Hawaii was annexed, about 1.8 million acres of land were taken from the Hawaiian monarchy by the US government and designated as "ceded lands." These lands are now held in trust for native Hawaiians and public use, and they are managed by organizations like the Office of Hawaiian Affairs (OHA). Ceded lands can only be used for public education, betterment of native Hawaiians, development of homes and farmsteads, public improvements like roads and parks, and other public uses like conservation, recreation, and affordable housing.[3]

Annexation also laid the groundwork for the Hawaiian Homes Commission Act of 1920, which set aside land for native Hawaiians. These homestead lands are leased to Hawaiians with at least 50% Hawaiian ancestry at affordable rates. While you can't invest directly in these lands unless you meet the criteria, knowing about the Hawaiian Homes Commission Act can help you navigate the local market.

Finally, annexation also paved the way for Hawaii to become a tourist destination, and the tourism industry has been a major force in Hawaii's real estate market ever since.

A PEOPLE DISPLACED

Hawaii became the 50th state in the United States in 1959, and everything changed again. It wasn't just a political shift. It was like flipping on a spotlight for the islands. Suddenly, the whole world wanted a piece of paradise, and that demand created a ripple effect across the real estate industry on every island. Tourism exploded, and hotels, resorts, and vacation homes started popping up everywhere.

When Hawaii became a state, it brought stability and credibility. Investors saw it as a safe place to put their money, and that confidence set the stage for massive development. Federal funding became available to build and improve airports, highways, and harbors. This made it easier for tourists and businesses to access the islands, fueling the demand for land. Hawaii's new status also made it more attractive to mainland buyers who wanted vacation homes or investments.

Statehood made land ownership rules clearer and more aligned with US property laws. This meant it became much easier for mainland investors to get involved in real estate investing in Hawaii. Ownership of land started to shift as large tracts of land once used for sugar and pineapple plantations started transitioning to urban developments, resorts, and housing.

I don't blame people for wanting to come to Hawaii. To me, it's the most beautiful place on Earth. Tourism is also great for the economy, especially in places like Waikiki and Maui. But tourism also brought concerns about overdevelopment, affecting the environment and local culture. Large-scale development has changed the landscape, and it's hard to see our land and culture pushed aside to make way for resorts and commercial projects sometimes. As investors, we've got a kuleana (responsibility) to respect the ʻāina (land) and the people who call it home—the Pono Way.

A CULTURE STILL HEALING

One of the biggest takeaways from the history of Hawaii's land is the concept of kuleana—the idea that each person has a responsibility to the land and community. Development here isn't just about profit. It's about respecting the cultural and environmental significance of the ʻāina (land). Many properties have ties to native Hawaiian history, whether it's an ancient burial site or a sacred location. Ignoring these ties can lead to community backlash—or worse, legal trouble.

Native Hawaiian culture is making a big comeback, and many people are working hard to reclaim the land and preserve our history. You can't approach investing in Hawaii like you would on the mainland. If you want to get into Hawaii real estate investing the Pono Way, you must appreciate that land is deeply tied to culture and identity.

Talk to locals and cultural experts to ensure the deals and projects you're considering respect native Hawaiian values and the land's heritage. Get to know how land-use laws, conservation preferences, and zoning mandates help you protect Hawaii's unique resources. I'll give you more specifics on navigating trusts, estates, leasehold properties, and zoning in the next chapter. But remember to always approach the land and locals with humility and a willingness to learn.

Hawaiian history teaches us that the land here isn't just property—it's part of a huge legacy. The laws, the culture, and even the people's approaches to deals are rooted in that history. If you want to succeed as a real estate investor the Pono Way, you've got to respect that. Learn the difference between leasehold and fee simple, understand zoning restrictions, and take the time to connect with the local community. When you approach investing in Hawaii with knowledge and respect, you're not only making a smart financial decision—you're becoming part of the story.

MAIN TAKEAWAYS FROM CHAPTER 8

1. **You can't invest in Hawaii without understanding its history.** If you're going to touch the land, you need to know the story behind it. Hawaii isn't just another place to do real estate—it's a kingdom that was overthrown, a people who were displaced, and a culture that's still healing. Respect starts with knowledge.

2. **The Great Māhele changed everything.** Back in 1848, the Great Māhele shifted land ownership from a communal, kingdom-based system to private property. That move opened the door for foreigners to own land and slowly pushed Hawaiians out of the very land they'd lived on for generations.

3. **Kuleana lands still matter today.** These are small parcels originally given to Hawaiian families—but over the years, many families lost their rights through legal loopholes and tax issues. Some of that land is still tied up in title disputes or managed by multiple descendants. If you don't know what you're doing, you can easily get caught up in a mess.

4. **The overthrow of the Hawaiian Kingdom left deep wounds.** When the US took over in 1893, it wasn't just political—it was personal. Hawaiians lost their sovereignty, their voice, and their control over the land. That pain still lives on today, and if you're investing here, you need to carry that awareness with you in every deal.

5. **Investing the Pono Way means doing your homework and leading with respect.** You're not just buying dirt— you're stepping into history. So slow down, learn, and lead with humility. When you understand the land's past, you'll know how to build a better future—for yourself and for Hawaii.

Chapter 9

The Other Side of Real Estate Investing in Hawaii

_____

I nvesting in Hawaii real estate isn't like investing anywhere else. You've read this far, so by now you know you can't just take what you know about the mainland market, drop it here, and expect it to work the same way. Hawaii is a whole different ball game.

In the last chapter, I gave you a rundown of Hawaii's history. Our land is more than geography. Our land has history and meaning, and it's tied to generations of families, to the culture, to the people. If you try to bulldoze through a deal without understanding that, you're gonna hit roadblocks—sometimes legal ones, sometimes spiritual ones, and sometimes ones that are just plain bad luck.

On top of that, Hawaii has some of the strictest zoning laws, the most unique ownership structures, and the biggest natural risks—things you won't find in most other markets.

Ever heard of a landlocked property? They exist here. Ever tried to build on land, only to find out there's a lava tube running underneath it? Here, it happens. Ever had a deal fall through because someone found *iwi* (human remains) during excavation? Yeah, that's a real thing, too.

That's why investing the Pono Way isn't just some feel-good idea. It's the only way that works here. You can't come in and think you'll play the market like a mainland investor chasing fast cash. You've got to respect the land, the people, and the process. When you do that, not only do the best deals find you, but you also build a real, lasting legacy.

In this chapter, I'm going to tell you all about the *other* side of Hawaii real estate. I'm talking about the challenges, the things nobody warns you about, and the mistakes that can cost you big time. But don't worry, I'm not here to scare you off. I'm here to make sure you walk into this market with your eyes wide open, so you can invest smart, invest strong, and invest the Pono Way.

ZONING CHALLENGES AND LAND USE RESTRICTIONS

One of the biggest mistakes new investors make in Hawaii is refusing to take the time to understand zoning laws before they buy a property. This isn't like buying a house on the mainland, where you assume you can do whatever you want with the land once you own it. In Hawaii, zoning laws can make or break your investment.

Agricultural and Conservation Land Restrictions

Hawaii is big on preserving its agricultural land, which means if you buy land zoned for agriculture, you can't just build a house on it. Some investors get excited about large plots of land, thinking they'll develop luxury homes, only to realize that legally, they can't.

Even if you're allowed to build, you might only be able to put up farm-related structures like barns or worker housing. If you're not actually farming the land, good luck getting approval to build anything residential.

Lesson to Learn: Just because land is cheap doesn't mean you can build on it. Always check zoning rules first.

ADUs (Accessory Dwelling Units)

For the investors who do their homework, zoning laws can create great opportunities. Some counties, like Maui and Hilo, have started allowing more Accessory Dwelling Units (ADUs). This means you can legally build extra rental units on certain residential properties. In Maui, some areas now allow two to three ADUs per property, depending on square footage. In Hilo, some properties can have up to three separate dwellings, making them a goldmine for rental income.

The housing shortage in Hawaii is real, so local governments are loosening restrictions to help. If you find a property that allows ADUs, you could build extra units, rent them out, and increase your cash flow, all while providing native Hawaiians with affordable places to live.

Lesson to Learn: Understanding local zoning laws can turn a basic property into a high-income investment.

Condominium Property Regime (CPR)

Another zoning trick savvy investors use is Condominium Property Regime (CPR). If a property has enough land, you might be able to legally split it into separate housing units with different addresses.

For example, let's say you buy a busted-up house with a big backyard. You could fix up the house and rent it out. While making rental income on the existing house, you check zoning regulations and realize you can use CPR and get permits to build two more homes in the back of the property. Once those are built, you sell or rent them separately.

This method lets you maximize value, increase cash flow, and refinance for more deals. Plus, it's another great way to provide affordable housing for Hawaiians!

Lesson to Learn: CPR can turn one deal into multiple income streams—but only if the zoning allows it.

Short-Term Rental Restrictions

Many areas, especially Honolulu and Maui, have cracked down on Airbnb and short-term vacation rentals. Some properties are in zones where vacation rentals are completely banned.

And don't expect you'll be able to change zones after you've purchased the property. It's not an easy process. Zoning changes require community input, environmental impact studies, and government approval.

Lesson to Learn: Always check zoning laws and permitted uses before buying.

The bottom line is that zoning can open doors...but it can also close them. If you know the rules, you can spot opportunities where others see obstacles. If you ignore the rules, you could end up stuck with land you can't use.

Ask these zoning questions before investing in Hawaii real estate:
- Can I legally build on it?
- If I can build, what exactly can I build?
- Are there restrictions on how I can use the land?
- Is the property landlocked?
- Are there ADU or CPR opportunities?
- Could this land have historical or sacred significance?

Where to Go with Land Restriction and Zoning Questions

For questions on zoning and land use restrictions, the best place to get answers is the Department of Planning and Permitting Office of the county the property is located in. Each island has its own county planning office that oversees zoning, permits, and building regulations. They can tell you the zoning designation of a property, what's allowed to be built there, whether you can add ADUs, if CPR is allowed, and clarify any other special restrictions. Architects who live in the area will also know what you can and can't build.

For questions on landlocked property, your best bet is to visit the County Property Tax Office and Public Records Office, where you can ask for property maps and surveys.

Visit the Tax Map Key (TMK) system online to learn about road access. You can also ask title companies if easements exist.

Investing the Pono Way means doing your due diligence, respecting the land, and making smart, informed decisions. If you take the time to understand zoning and land use restrictions, you can avoid costly mistakes and set yourself up for long-term success.

LEASEHOLD VS. FEE SIMPLE

One of the biggest ways Hawaii's real estate market is different from the mainland is Hawaii's leasehold structure. This can be a big challenge for a real estate investor, so understanding the difference between leasehold and fee simple ownership is important. If you don't know what you're getting into, you could end up with a property you don't really own.

Fee Simple Ownership

Fee simple ownership is what most people think of when they buy property. When you buy, you own the land and any structures on it outright until you decide to sell. There are no time limits or conditions beyond standard property taxes and regulations with fee simple ownership. If you buy a fee simple property in Hawaii, it's yours to live in, rent out, or sell at any time. You can also pass it down to your children and grandchildren, and you are free to develop it as long as it's in a zone that allows the kind of development you intend.

Basically, fee simple is full ownership. It's just like buying a house on the mainland, and it is the most secure and valuable form of ownership in Hawaii. But here's the catch: Hawaii has a limited supply of fee simple land and a LOT of leasehold land, especially in desirable areas like Honolulu, Maui, and Kona. Because demand is so high and availability is so low, fee simple properties can be extremely expensive.

Leasehold Ownership

Leasehold is like long-term renting, where you own the structure but not the dirt under it. When a piece of land is under leasehold ownership, the land itself can't be bought, but the houses, condos, or other buildings that sit on it can. The land is then leased from the leasehold owner for a set period, usually 30, 50, or 99 years.

Leasehold properties can allow you to purchase homes at lower upfront purchase prices because you're not buying the land. During the lease, you'll pay the mortgage for the land and monthly lease rent payments. Paying less for properties sounds great, but leasehold deals come with their own set of challenges.

The lease will eventually expire. Once the lease term is up, all bets may be off. Best case scenario, the landowner could extend the terms of the lease with you. But if the landowner chooses not to renew, you will lose the property and any investment you put into it.

The lease rent could increase. Many leasehold properties have escalation clauses, which means the lease payments will go up over time, sometimes dramatically. If the land value rises, the lease rent could, too.

Appreciation is limited. One of the things that makes real estate such a great investment is that land is an asset that appreciates over time. But under leasehold, you don't own the land, so a leasehold property doesn't gain value the way fee simple properties do. When the lease gets closer to expiration, the property's value will drop sharply.

Financing can be challenging. Most banks won't offer 30-year mortgages on a leasehold property with less than 30 years left on the lease. If the lease has fewer than 10 years left, financing is nearly impossible, so you may have to get creative with your funding sources.

All in all, leasehold properties can be great for short-term income, but they are risky for long-term investment. Here's an example of what I mean:

Let's say you buy a leasehold condo in Waikiki. The price is great—way cheaper than a fee simple condo in the same area. You decide to rent it out, and you're making good money.

But ten years later, when the lease runs out, the landowner decides not to renew the lease as is. Instead, they want to renegotiate the lease, and because the land value has appreciated over time, the rent the leasehold owner wants now is so high it kills your profits. If you can't pay, you'll lose the property entirely and be left with nothing to show for the investment you made. Unfortunately, this happens all the time in Hawaii, and uninformed investors lose big.

If the landowner decides to sell the land, however, leaseholders may have the chance to buy it and convert it to fee simple…but I wouldn't count on that happening. First of all, it depends on who owns the land. Much of Hawaii's leasehold land is owned by trusts and estates that will never sell. Second, it could be too costly to buy, especially if the land is in a really desirable location. Finally, some homeowners associations don't allow for land to be converted from leasehold to fee simple. Before buying a leasehold property, ask if conversion is an option. If not, make sure you have a solid exit strategy and proceed with caution.

Who Owns Most of the Leasehold Land in Hawaii?

Many leasehold properties in Hawaii are controlled by the Bishop Estate, which runs the Kamehameha Schools. They're one of the largest private landowners in Hawaii, and rarely sell their land, meaning leaseholders stay stuck in lease agreements.

Another group that owns a lot of leasehold properties is the Department of Hawaiian Home Lands (DHHL). The DHHL offers 99-year leaseholds for native Hawaiians. If you're at least 50% Hawaiian, you can request an application packet through the DHHL. The application will show you how to put your name on the list, get qualified, go through courses, and qualify for a loan. These leaseholds come with ultra-low lease rents, such as $1 per year. These leases can be passed down to children and grandchildren, but they're not available to non-Hawaiians.

Finally, there are some estates and corporations that own large amounts of Hawaiian land and choose to lease it out rather than sell. These can be unpredictable because some sell, some don't.

Should You Invest in Leasehold Properties?

The question of whether to purchase under leasehold is one to carefully consider. My best advice is if you're looking for a long-term investment, fee simple is always safer. But if you understand the risks and have an exit plan, leasehold can be a good short-term opportunity. Use this chart to help you weigh leasehold opportunities.

Consider Leasehold If...	Walk Away If...
• You're looking for a lower upfront investment. • You only plan to hold the property short-term. • You understand the lease terms and renewal risks. • You're okay with rising lease rent payments. • You can buy cash or secure financing (some banks won't lend).	• The lease is under 30 years (banks won't finance). • There's no chance to buy the land and convert to fee simple. • You're looking for long-term appreciation. • The lease rent will increase too fast and seriously eat into your profits.

Thinking about purchasing leasehold property? Ask these questions:
- How many years are left on the lease?
- How much is the lease rent, and how often does it go up?
- What happens when the lease expires?
- Can I buy the land and convert it to fee simple?
- Will banks finance this property, or do I need cash?

Don't jump into a leasehold property without knowing the risks. If you're smart and do your due diligence, you can still make leasehold work, but only if it fits your strategy.

NATURAL DISASTERS AND GEOLOGICAL RISKS

Hawaii might be paradise, but it's also one of the most geologically active and environmentally vulnerable places on Earth. If you're investing in Hawaii real estate, you must understand the natural risks that come with it. Hawaii has active volcanoes, earthquakes, tsunamis, coastal erosion, and even hidden lava tubes. These events can destroy a property overnight or make getting insurance nearly impossible. Let's talk about each of these disasters and risks, because knowing how to navigate them can make a huge difference in your real estate investing journey.

Lava Zones and Volcanic Activity

The Hawaiian Islands are made up of a chain of volcanoes, some of which are still very much active. If you're buying property here, you need to understand Hawaii's lava zones.

The Big Island is the only Hawaiian island with active volcanoes, and it's divided into nine lava zones. Lava zones 1 and 2 are the high-risk zones with frequent lava flows. If a massive eruption happens, your property could be buried in lava overnight. It's very hard to get homeowners insurance in zones 1 and 2. You also need to keep in mind that the state won't rebuild infrastructure in high-risk zones, so you may be stuck with no help if roads, water lines, or utilities are wiped out.

Lava zones 3 and 4 are the moderate risk zones. Some properties in these zones sit on old lava flows, making "solid ground" not so solid. These areas have had historical volcanic activity, but they aren't currently active. Lava zones 5–9 are low risk and contain minimal volcanic threats.

I remember witnessing Kilauea erupt as a young kid in the 1980s. You could see the red lava shooting hundreds of feet into the air. Natives said it was Pele, the lava goddess. Lava debris, called Pele's hair, littered the ground and covered people's roofs. Ash fell into the water, and the sky was covered in volcanic fog, or vog.

In 2018, Kilauea erupted in Leilani Estates and destroyed 700+ homes overnight, covering 14 square miles with lava that was 30 feet high in some places. People lost everything, and some had no insurance because they were in a high-risk zone. If you're considering land in a lava-prone area, do your research. The cheaper price might not be worth the risk. You can learn more about the lava risk on a specific piece of land through Hawaii County Lava Zone Maps or by asking insurance providers about a property before buying.

Lava Tubes

Even if you're not in an active lava zone, you could still have a lava tube problem. Lava tubes are underground tunnels left behind by old lava flows. They might be hidden under a property, just waiting to cause all kinds of problems.

You can't build over lava tubes. Not only is it unstable, but your building permits could be denied because of the related safety issues if a lava tube is found on your property. The ground could unexpectedly collapse, leading to dangerous sinkholes. You don't want to end up one of those investors who buys a piece of land and starts to clear it, only to later discover a massive lava tube hidden beneath the surface.

Before buying land, walk the property and look for sinkholes and uneven ground—both of which can be big red flags. Don't forget to ask the landowner about past lava activity and check property surveys and geological maps.

Earthquakes

Volcanic activity and earthquakes tend to go hand in hand, and that's definitely true in Hawaii. Hawaii has frequent earthquakes, especially on the Big Island where earthquakes can be signs of potential eruptions. For example, in 2006, a 6.7 magnitude earthquake hit the Big Island, causing millions in damage to homes and roads.

As a real estate investor, you need to be aware that older buildings may not be earthquake-proof and may need extensive renovation or risk becoming damaged if an earthquake occurs. Check if the property you're looking at is in a high seismic zone, especially if you're considering purchasing an older home. Consider buying only properties built after 1990, when modern earthquake codes were enforced, and check whether the area qualifies for earthquake insurance. If not, you may want to look elsewhere.

Tsunamis

In addition to being a hotbed for volcanic activity and earthquakes, Hawaii is in the middle of the Pacific Ocean. Tsunamis are always a possibility when there's seismic activity. Coastal properties in tsunami zones are high-risk investments, and if a tsunami destroys your property, rebuilding may not be allowed. Tsunami evacuation zones also impact property values and insurance rates.

In 1946, a tsunami wiped out most of downtown Hilo, killing 159 people. Today, Hilo remains one of the most tsunami-prone areas in Hawaii. Before buying oceanfront property, check if it's in a tsunami evacuation zone and proceed with caution. To find out whether a property is at risk for tsunamis, check Hawaii Tsunami Evacuation Zone Maps and ask your insurance provider about flood and tsunami coverage.

Coastal Erosion

Last but not least, remember that if you're buying near the ocean, rising sea levels and erosion could wipe out your investment. Under Special Management Area rules, you can't build closer than 40 feet to the shoreline. If the ocean takes your land, you can't rebuild. Your property is gone, period.

In 2021, massive erosion forced multiple homes to collapse into the ocean along Oahu's North Shore. Homeowners were not allowed to rebuild, and this still happens today. I saw an article in the *New York Post* that talked about a homeowner who purchased some oceanfront property in 2021 on Oahu's North Shore for $1,000,000. Despite efforts to mitigate erosion, his home collapsed into the ocean in 2024, resulting in a total loss.[1]

Oceanfront property can be risky. Always check erosion rates before buying, by looking at Hawaii coastal erosion maps and consulting a structural engineer before buying oceanfront property. Hawaii's beauty comes with risks. If you don't do your research, you could end up with a property that's uninsurable or unlivable—or worse, is destined to be washed away in the next disaster.

Before you invest, ask these questions:
- What lava zone is this property in?
- Are there any indications that lava tubes might be beneath the land?
- Is this property in a tsunami or flood zone?
- Is there a history of earthquakes in this area?
- What's the erosion rate?
- Can I get insurance?

The best investors in Hawaii don't just chase deals. They respect the land, understand the risks, and make educated decisions. If you invest wisely, you'll reap the rewards. If you ignore these risks, you could lose everything.

CULTURAL AND HISTORICAL CONSIDERATIONS

Hawaiian land has history, spirit, and meaning. If you don't understand that, you will run into problems. I grew up next to a *heiau*—a Hawaiian temple. It was one of those places you *knew* not to mess with. As kids, we were told stories about *Menehune* (little people) and spirits that would walk the land at night. People would warn, *"Don't take rocks from the heiau, don't disturb the land, and definitely don't build on sacred ground."*

There are sacred places like this all over the islands, but, of course, not everyone listens to or respects the cultural and spiritual traditions of Hawaii. Foreign developers come in and push bulldozers through sacred sites like they're nothing. I've seen what happens when people ignore the history of the land, and it never ends well.

There's a reason why some places feel *off*. If you try to develop land with history—Hawaiian trails, burial sites, old heiau—you're asking for trouble. And I don't just mean from the county or historic preservation boards, though that's a whole mess on its own. Sometimes the trouble might come in ways you can't always see with your eyes.

Hawaiian Trails and Sacred Paths

Before paved roads and cars existed on the islands, Hawaiians walked the land on sacred trails that connected the mountains to the sea and settlements to each other. Some of these paths were used by *ali'i* (chiefs) or *huaka'i pō* (warriors) for sacred journeys. Others were more common routes for families traveling across the islands.[3]

Those paths are still here, although many have fallen out of use. Outsiders buy land without realizing the spiritual and historical significance these trails have. Sometimes they build right over the top of them. It might not seem like that big a deal, but I've heard stories.

According to legend, if you build over one of these sacred trails, don't be surprised if you get visitors, and not the kind that will walk up and knock on your door. People talk about seeing shadowy figures moving at night, hearing chanting, or feeling a presence in the room. Some say they're being visited by night marchers—spirits of ancient warriors who are still walking their path.

If you're investing in Hawaii real estate, make sure you're *not* buying on an ancient trail, especially if you're the superstitious kind, unless you're comfortable with a little extra company.

Iwi Kūpuna

On a more serious note, there are times when caring for the sacred is more than just respecting superstition. *Iwi kūpuna* means bones of ancestors. The islands are home to many ancestral Hawaiian burial sites, and they're not always well-marked.

This is a *huge* issue in Hawaii, especially for developers. You buy land and start excavation, thinking everything will go according to plan…until you unearth human bones. Then everything stops. Construction must pause while the State Historic Preservation Division (SHPD) and Hawaiian cultural organizations step in to decide what happens next.

That's inconvenient and costly in terms of time and often money. Sometimes developers try to push through by hiding the bones and not reporting the *iwi*. That's when projects fall apart, deals collapse, and workers refuse to step on site.

That's not the Pono Way. Do your best to research the property for historical sites and burial grounds. If iwi are found, handle the situation with respect. Work with Hawaiian cultural leaders. *Do not* bulldoze over sacred history.

Hawaiian Temples and Sacred Sites

Like I said, I grew up next to a heiau. These aren't just old ruins. They're seen as powerful places in Hawaiian culture.

Some heiau were for healing, others for agriculture, and some were even used for sacrifices. Hawaiians believe that messing with a heiau can bring serious consequences.

I've seen people take rocks from heiau or volcanic areas as souvenirs. Next thing you know, they're mailing them back to Hawaii because their life started falling apart. This happens *all the time*. Look it up—there are boxes of rocks returned every year to the National Park Service because people swear they bring bad luck. I saw a YouTube video about how Haleakalā National Park on Maui reported receiving 1,275 rocks returned by mail in a single year.[2]

If you find a property near a heiau, respect it. Don't build over it, don't take anything from it, and definitely don't disturb it.

Oceanfront Land and Hawaiian Legends

Even the ocean has its rules in Hawaii. Some lands are tied to old Hawaiian legends about places where gods and spirits still roam. One of the biggest cultural no-nos is blocking access to the ocean.

Hawaiians have always had the right to fish, gather, and travel along the shorelines. But some wealthy investors try to build fences and private walls, cutting off public access. Legally, it's against the law to block public access to the ocean. Culturally, it's even worse.

There's a saying here: If you disrespect the ocean, the ocean will take your land. And trust me, I've seen it happen. Coastal erosion, high surf, and King Tides have caused whole sections of beachfront homes to disappear into the sea. Coincidence? Maybe. But in Hawaii, we know better.

Before you invest, ask these questions:
- Does this property sit on or near a heiau (sacred temple)?
- Are there any known iwi kūpuna (human remains) in or near this property?
- Could this land be part of an ancient Hawaiian trail?
- Would my development plans block access to the ocean, fishing areas, or gathering places?

COMMERCIAL PROPERTY INVESTMENT CHALLENGES

Investing in commercial real estate in Hawaii can be a game changer. More doors can equal more cash flow and tax benefits, but it also comes with unique risks. The Hawaiian commercial real estate market is heavily regulated, expensive, and competitive, making it harder to get into.

That doesn't mean you shouldn't give commercial real estate a shot, though. Whether you're looking at strip malls, office buildings, short-term rentals, or industrial properties, you need to be aware of the challenges that could drain your investment before you ever see a profit. Let's talk about some of those challenges.

High Costs and Limited Inventory
Unlike the mainland, where you can find large parcels for industrial parks or retail centers, Hawaii's geography limits commercial real estate options, even though there's a great

need for it. Add in high construction costs, and investing in the commercial market can get tricky.

Buying commercial property in prime locations like Honolulu, Waikiki, or Maui can cost millions. Even in less tourist-heavy areas, prices are high due to land scarcity. Because Hawaii is an island chain, there's only so much land available. That means the few commercial properties on the market face stiff competition from big investors.

Building new commercial space costs significantly more in Hawaii than on the mainland, due to material import costs and strict regulations. If you're looking at commercial real estate, be prepared to pay premium prices and compete with major investors.

Leasehold vs. Fee Simple

Commercial real estate is another place where Hawaii's leasehold ownership comes into play. Most mainland commercial real estate is fee simple, while many of Hawaii's commercial properties are leasehold. So, you may own the building, but you're leasing the land from another entity, like the Bishop Estate or Kamehameha Schools. Once the lease expires, the landowner can refuse to renew your lease and force you out. They can also raise lease payments, cutting into your profits.

Plus, just like with residential situations, if a lease has less than 30 years left, getting a loan is nearly impossible. If you invest in commercial property, make sure the lease has enough years left to make it worth it. Otherwise, you're playing a dangerous game.

Commercial Zoning and Permitting Nightmares

Hawaii has some of the strictest zoning laws in the US, and changing a property's use often takes considerable time. That means if you want to buy residential or agricultural property and convert it into commercial, you have a long, uphill climb ahead of you. Permitting can take months or even years, and some businesses (like vacation rentals) are banned in certain zones.

And don't assume a commercial property can be used for anything. Just because a building looks like it could be a great retail space doesn't mean it's legally allowed. Zoning changes require community input. In Hawaii, locals fight hard against developments they don't like. Before investing, check zoning laws, and don't assume you can easily convert a property to commercial zoning.

High Vacancy Rates

While tourism and retail are strong in places like Waikiki, other areas struggle with high vacancy rates. Some commercial spaces sit empty for months or years if there isn't enough demand. Common high-vacancy areas include older office buildings in Honolulu, strip malls and shopping centers outside major tourist zones, and industrial spaces. If you invest in the wrong location, you could struggle to find tenants. Hawaii has very few large-scale manufacturing businesses, so demand for warehouse space isn't as high as in other states.

A commercial building that sits empty is a money pit, and if your tenants leave, you could go months without rental income. Research market demand before buying. If businesses aren't thriving in the area, your property won't either. To check vacancy rates in specific areas, look at *Hawaii Business Magazine* and local real estate reports like CBRE Group (formerly known as Coldwell Banker Richard Ellis), Colliers, and Jones Lang LaSalle (JLL).

Market Dependence on Tourism

Hawaii's economy is heavily dependent on tourism. If tourism declines, commercial businesses are the first to suffer. When tourism drops, hotels, restaurants, and retail spaces struggle. COVID-19 showed us how fragile the market is, as many Hawaiian businesses shut down permanently. Anytime there are cruise ship bans or reduced flights, there are fewer visitors to Hawaii. This hurts retail investors like shopping centers, small businesses, restaurant owners, and short-term rental operators. A good rule of thumb is if you invest in commercial real estate, make sure it's not 100% reliant on tourism.

Commercial Property in Hawaii Isn't for Beginners

Commercial real estate in Hawaii can be lucrative, but it's not easy. If you don't understand the risks, you could end up paying premium prices for a property you can't rent, develop, or finance.

Before you invest in commercial real estate, ask these questions:

- Is this property leasehold or fee simple? If it's leasehold, how many years are left?
- Can I legally use this building the way I want to?
- Is there demand for businesses in this area?
- What happens if tourism drops?
- Can I get financing?

ETHICAL CONSIDERATIONS IN REAL ESTATE INVESTING

Real estate investing isn't just about making money—it's about *how* you make money. In Hawaii, where land has deep cultural and historical significance, how you conduct business matters as much as the deals you close.

Some investors come in with a mainland mentality. They see a distressed property, a struggling family, or a foreclosed home, and all they think about is profit. They forget that these properties aren't only assets on a spreadsheet. They're homes. They have history. And when you treat people like numbers, you don't just lose deals. You lose respect.

That's why I believe in investing the Pono Way. When you do things the right way, with integrity and respect, the land takes care of you. Here are some ways to make sure you're investing the Pono Way.

Foreclosures That Exploit Homeowners

Foreclosures happen everywhere, but in Hawaii, they hit differently. Many homes here have been in Hawaiian families for generations. Losing them isn't just financial. It's a cultural loss, too.

Unfortunately, some real estate investors take advantage of desperate homeowners. They rush in, offer pennies on the dollar, and leave families with nothing. Instead of explaining all the possibilities available, some investors push sellers into lowball deals they don't fully understand.

Another way some real estate investors exploit people in foreclosure is by offering cash- for-keys deals while giving families little time to relocate. The families take the deal, thinking it's a godsend, only to realize they're left without anywhere to go.

This one hits close to home for me. I got into real estate because I saw my own family go through foreclosure. I saw how helpless they felt, how unfair the process seemed, and how no one took the time to explain their options to them. That really stuck with me.

When I do business, I ask myself: Would I do this deal if it was my mom's house? My sister's house? If the answer is no, I don't do it. At the end of the day, real estate isn't just about numbers. It's about people, history, culture, and community. And if you can't do business the Pono Way, you shouldn't do business here at all.

How to Invest in Foreclosures the RIGHT Way

Instead of exploiting homeowners in foreclosure, you can be part of the solution! Here's how:

First, make sure you come ready to educate homeowners about their options, and I mean ALL their options. If they can refinance, apply for assistance, or work out a loan modification instead of selling at a loss—tell them.

Second, offer fair deals. If you're profiting from their loss, at least make it a win-win by being fair and ensuring they walk away happy. And give them time to move. If they need to sell, you can help them transition, instead of just taking the keys and booting them out.

Clear Title Concerns

I mentioned kuleana lands earlier in this chapter, but there's one more consideration to make when it comes to these properties granted to native Hawaiian families in the mid-1800s. They come with major legal and ethical implications that you need to be aware of.

Kuleana lands are often co-owned by many descendants, some of whom don't even know they have ownership rights. If you buy kuleana land, you could end up in a long legal battle over ownership. Buying out one family member's share doesn't always mean you own the land. It just means you have a piece of a family's heritage. So how do you handle kuleana lands the right way?

I recommend only making deals on land with clear titles. If there are multiple family members involved, talk to everyone, not just one seller. And know when to walk away. Getting a good deal isn't worth causing issues that could separate a family.

The Affordable Housing Shortage

Hawaii has one of the worst housing crises in the US. In 2023, only 20% of local households could afford a mortgage on a median-priced, single-family home in Hawaii.[4] Investors play a role in the housing situation, whether they want to or not. It's up to you whether you play a positive or negative role.

Some investors worsen the housing crisis by buying affordable homes, flipping them, and pricing out locals. Others turn long-term rentals into Airbnbs or Vrbos, reducing the supply of housing available for people who live here. Still others come in and gentrify neighborhoods, forcing local families to leave.

Instead of being like those real estate investors, be part of the solution. Consider renting to locals, not just high-paying tourists. If you're flipping, don't price out the local market. And work with community programs to create housing solutions. The great thing is, you can make money without making the Hawaiian housing crisis worse.

Work With, Not Against, the Local Community

Some investors fight the community instead of working with them, and that's a big mistake. The local community can be a huge support, or they can make things difficult. It's up to you which way it goes.

Don't come in and start developing without getting community input. You don't want to start pushing projects locals don't want. Remember, these people will be your neighbors. You can't treat Hawaii like you treat other markets. Instead, go to local meetings, listen to the people there—get input. Support community projects instead of just making money from them, and hire local workers and contractors. That's how to gain community support.

Before you invest, ask these questions to ensure you're doing things ethically:

- Am I helping or hurting the people involved?
- Is this deal fair to everyone involved?
- Am I respecting the land and its history?
- Would I do this if it was my own family's home?

TAX AND LEGAL CHALLENGES

Hawaii is paradise...but it's also one of the most heavily regulated and taxed states in the US. If you don't understand the legal and tax implications before investing, you could end up losing money, fighting legal battles, or dealing with a property you can't even sell.

Some investors rush into deals without researching the tax and legal structure. They find themselves stuck with unexpected costs, title disputes, or government red tape that can delay their projects for months or even years. If you're investing in Hawaii real estate, here are the tax and legal challenges you need to watch out for.

Hawaii's Unique Property Tax System

Hawaii has some of the lowest property tax rates in the US, but that doesn't mean you're off the hook. Depending on how you use your property, you could get hit with higher tax rates or penalties. And unless you live in the home, you shouldn't expect to get a Hawaii homeowners tax exemption. Here are some key property tax considerations investors need to be aware of:

Owner-Occupied vs. Non-Owner-Occupied Tax Rates
If you live in the home, you'll pay lower residential property taxes. If you rent it out or use it as an investment, you'll pay higher non-owner-occupied tax rates.

Vacation Rentals and Hotel Taxes Some counties charge higher property tax rates on vacation rentals, like Airbnbs. This is to discourage investors from taking housing away from locals. If you rent your property for fewer than 180 days per tenant, you may owe Transient Accommodations Tax (TAT) and General Excise Tax (GET).

Commercial vs. Residential Property Taxes Commercial properties are taxed at higher rates than residential properties. If you try to convert a residential home into a business or vacation rental, you may see your tax bill double or triple.

Before buying, check the property tax classification—because changing how you use the property could change how much you owe. You can check Hawaiian property tax rates by going into the county office or by looking at the county property tax offices' websites.

Landlocked Properties
Imagine buying what looks like a steal of a property—cheap price, great location—only to find out there's no legal way to access it. That's what we call a landlocked property. When a piece of land is completely surrounded by other private properties, you might have to convince one of the private property owners to sell you a strip of their land for access. And guess what? They're not legally obligated to sell it to you. If they don't want to sell or allow land access, you might be stuck with a beautiful but useless piece of property.

If the price looks too good to be true, check access rights before making an offer. In a landlocked situation, it might be more of a headache than it's worth if you can't even get into the property.

Sacred Land & Iwi (Human Remains)

Like I mentioned before, one of the most serious challenges real estate investors face in Hawaii is accidentally buying land with sacred history. If you start excavation and find iwi (human remains), the whole project comes to a halt. The land could be deemed sacred, and depending on what's found, you might never be able to build there.

Some locals will tell you horror stories of developers ignoring these warnings, only to suffer massive financial losses, or worse, personal misfortunes. The Hawaiian community takes disrespecting sacred land seriously, and if you choose to treat sacred land without consideration, this can lead to bad blood, bad press, and—many people believe—bad luck.

Always research the land's history before buying it. If iwi are found, respect the process and work with cultural experts to honor the deceased the right way.

Hawaii's Tax Deed & Foreclosure Laws

Buying a foreclosed property in Hawaii isn't as simple as bidding at an auction, but tax deed auctions can be great ways to open up deals. Here's how purchasing a tax deed works in Hawaii:

If a property owner fails to pay property taxes for three years, the county can auction off the tax deed. Tax deed auctions are advertised publicly, and anyone can attend. But winning a tax auction doesn't mean you own the property immediately. The original owner has one year to buy it back, by paying the back taxes plus 1% interest per month.[5]

This means as the investor, you may not get possession of a tax lien property for a year. You'll also need to hire a lawyer to clear any title disputes. Plus, some tax lien properties have existing tenants, so you might also have to go through eviction proceedings. Buying foreclosures in Hawaii takes time, legal fees, and patience…but it can be a great way to get a good deal on a property.

You can check for foreclosures and tax deed sales on the Hawaii County Tax Auctions website, listed in the Resources section of this book.

Beyond Property Taxes

In addition to property taxes, Hawaii real estate investors are hit with additional taxes (a few of which I mentioned already) that can eat into profits. It's important to know what these taxes are, so you can be prepared. Here are the additional taxes to look out for:

General Excise Tax (GET) This tax applies to rental income, house flipping profits, and commercial leases, and is between 4% to 4.5%.

Transient Accommodations Tax (TAT) If you rent out a property for less than 180 days, you must pay TAT + GET taxes, which together are 10.25%.

Capital Gains Tax (State) + Federal Capital Gains If you sell a property and make a profit, you owe Hawaii state capital gains tax + federal capital gains tax up to 7.25%.

HARPTA (Hawaii Real Property Tax Act) If you're not a Hawaii resident and sell property, the state automatically withholds 7.25% from the sale price for taxes.

You can learn more on the Hawaii Department of Taxation website listed in the Resources section.

Before you invest, ask these questions to make sure you're prepared for taxes:

- What taxes will I owe on rental income?
- Am I legally allowed to use this property the way I want?
- Is this property in foreclosure?
- What are my capital gains tax obligations if I sell?

The Rewards of Investing the Pono Way

Hawaii real estate isn't just another market. It's a place of history, culture, and deep personal connection for the people who live here. The land isn't just property. It's a legacy, a resource, and a responsibility.

Too many investors come in blind, chasing fast money, and treating Hawaii like it's just another investment. They see distressed properties and undervalued land, but they don't see the families fighting to keep their homes, the cultural significance of the land, or the long-term impact their actions will have. And that's where they go wrong. Because Hawaii isn't like the mainland. If you don't respect the land, the land won't respect you.

When you invest the Pono Way, taking the time to learn the laws, respect the land, and help people, Hawaii opens up opportunities you won't find anywhere else, like:

- Long-term financial growth in a market where land is limited and values tend to rise
- The support of the local community because you're doing business ethically
- Unique investment opportunities like ADUs, CPR projects, and tax advantages for long-term rentals
- A deeper connection to the land and its people

When you invest the Pono Way, you're not just making money, you're building something meaningful. The investors who understand that are the ones who succeed.

MAIN TAKEAWAYS FROM CHAPTER 9

1. **Real estate investing has a dark side in Hawaii.** Let's not sugarcoat it—there are investors out here who don't care about the culture or the people or the damage they're doing. They buy land just to flip it fast, jack up rents, and cash out—leaving locals priced out and communities broken. That's not how we do things the Pono Way.

2. **Zoning laws in Hawaii are strict and can stop your project before it starts.** Just because land is for sale doesn't mean you can do what you want with it. Hawaii has serious zoning rules—especially around shoreline access, agriculture, and cultural sites. You've got to know what's allowed before you buy, or you could get stuck.

3. **Natural disasters are part of life in the islands.** From lava zones on the Big Island to floods on Kauai and hurricanes across the state, you have to factor in disaster risk. Insurance isn't cheap—or even available—and one bad storm can wipe out a project if you're not prepared.

4. **Titles in Hawaii can get complicated—fast.** Between kuleana lands, family ownership, and unclear records, title issues are common here. You've got to do your due diligence and work with a solid title company to ensure you're not stepping into a legal mess.

5. **Property taxes can crush you if you're not paying attention.** When values rise, so do taxes—and for families who've owned property for generations, that can be devastating. As an investor, you need to understand how taxes work and how to structure your deals so they don't backfire on you or the people living in one of the properties you invest in.

---

6. **Investing the Pono Way means seeing the whole picture.** It's not just about the deal. It's about the history, the people, the rules, and the land itself. When you slow down, stay informed, and lead with intention, you can build something that makes money *and* makes a difference.

PART 4

The Plan

Chapter 10

Build Your Real Estate Investing Business Plan

Congrats! It's time to start building your real estate investing business. I want to help you get off to the best start possible. So, before you head out to Drive for Dollars, put up bandit signs, or place a Craigslist ad, let's get you set up for success with some quick action steps.

In this chapter, I'm going to walk you through how to build a strong foundation for your business from day one by uncovering your deep "why," so you can set goals, get your finances in order, and make a plan to improve your credit score (if needed). As you read through the action prompts in this chapter, write down your answers as you go. I've created a downloadable Getting Started Guide you can use to record your progress. To access it, visit the book web page at https://huimastermind.com/case-study-3-ways-to-start.

UNCOVERING YOUR DEEP "WHY"

Remember when I talked about how important it is to have a deep "why" in chapter 6? It's time for you to do a little digging to uncover your personal deep "why" in the following pages. Ask yourself the following questions, then fill in the space below or in the Getting Started Guide.

What things in life do I value the most? List at least three things.

Why do I value those things?

What will real estate investing allow me to do/be/become?

Why do I want to do/be/become those things?

> [empty box]

What will my day-to-day life look like when I achieve those things?

> [empty box]

Now take your answers to the previous five questions and create a statement that explains your deep "why." Record it in the space below (or in your guide):

My Deep "Why" Is:

> [empty box]

When your "why" is strong enough, no setback or fear can hold you back. Write it down, post it on your mirror or make it a screensaver for your computer or phone. Trust me, uncovering your deep "why" is an important part of investing in real estate the Pono Way and will be the foundation for everything you'll build in this business and in this life.

SETTING REAL ESTATE GOALS

The first thing you need to do when setting goals based on your deep "why" is decide what you want to accomplish this year in real estate investing. Check or circle the goals you want to achieve here or in the Getting Started Guide:

- Buy my first Hawaiian property
- Replace the income from my current job
- Learn how to flip a home
- Make an extra $50k this year
- Grow my rental portfolio
- Passively invest in property
- Other _____

Next, narrow it down to one main goal you can start with, and write it in the space below (or in your guide).

GOAL #1

Reverse engineer how you'll go from where you are today to your goal by breaking down the big goal into individual steps you need to take.

_____

_____

_____

_____

_____

_____

_____

SETTING LIFE GOALS

Now, think back to your "why." There's a reason you want to start investing in Hawaii real estate, and I'm guessing it has something to do with the kind of lifestyle you want to live and the way you want to spend your time. Those are important life goals that will help keep you motivated when things get tough. Write down the life goals you want to achieve below or in the Getting Started Guide—these are the goals that investing in Hawaii real estate will help you reach.

Family Goals

```



```

Health Goals

```



```

Recreation Goals

Spirituality Goals

Friendship Goals

Environmental Goals

Next, choose one of the above life goals to start with, and write it in the space below or in the Getting Started Guide.

GOAL #2

Reverse engineer how you'll achieve this life goal by breaking down this big, life goal into individual steps you'll take. Write them below or in the Getting Started Guide.

_____

_____

_____

_____

_____

_____

_____

Now block out some time in your calendar to take action on each of the steps for your real estate and life goals. Track your progress along the way and share your goals with an accountability partner! You're not in this alone. Investing the Pono Way means building a balanced, integrity-filled life. It's not just about real estate investing, it's about working together with others and helping each other out like a family does.

ASSESSING YOUR FINANCES

Before you can start investing, you need to get clear on your finances, so you can figure out what you'll need in terms of financing. That way, you'll know which real estate strategies you want to start with.

Step 1: Identify Your Quadrant

I remember reading the book *Rich Dad Poor Dad* by Robert Kiyosaki when I was in prison. In the book, there was a chart that looked like this, which described four ways to generate income:

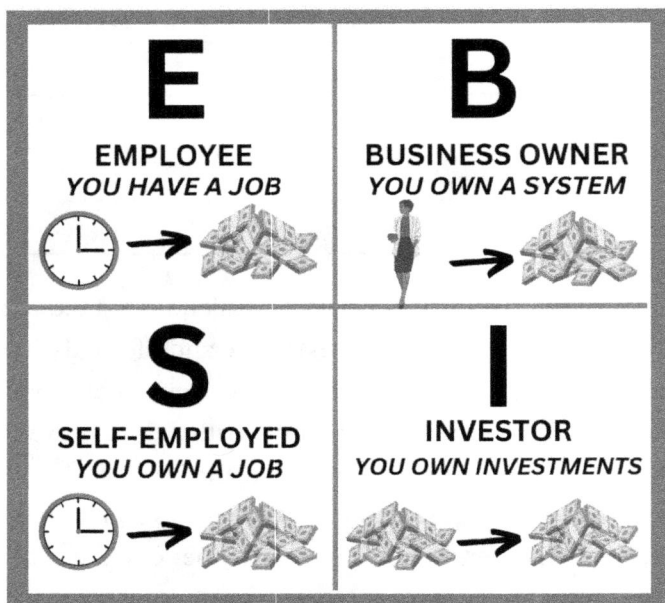

Once I got out of prison, I spent several years solidly in the employee category. I worked way too many hours a week, holding down as many as three jobs at a time. I was tired of trading my time for dollars and knew I was never going to get ahead like I wanted unless I started doing something different. I knew I wanted to move into the investor category.

Now it's your turn. Using the chart below, record your answers to the following questions here or in the Getting Started Guide.

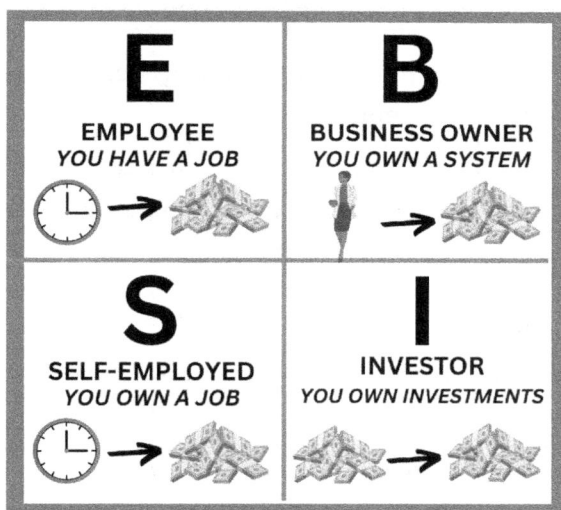

Which quadrant are you currently in? _____

Which quadrant would you like to be in? _____

Now, let's create the path to get where you want to be!

Step 2: Track Your Income and Expenses
In the beginning, my goal was to make $10,000 a month in passive income. That's what I knew it would take for my

family to be financially comfortable, and for me to create more free time to spend time with my wife and kids. Back then, $10,000 seemed like a pretty big goal. I knew I needed to break down the goal to getting there, so I could take action one step at a time.

The first thing I did was write down my income and all my expenses. Then I went through my expenses and tightened things up. I discovered that by trimming my expenses, I could save about $1,000 a month. That was great, but it was a long way from $10,000. To reach my goal, I needed to increase my income by $9,000 a month.

Now it's your turn. When it comes to your finances, be realistic about where you are now and figure out what resources you will need to reach your financial goal. To fund your first deals, you need to take stock of your assets and spending, and you have to know your actual income—whether that's from savings, a job, or a side hustle. You also need to know your expenses.

Record your income and monthly expenses like rent, mortgage, utilities, insurance, and daycare, so you can see where your finances are right now. You can use the space below or write it all down in the Getting Started Guide. I've also left some blank spaces for you to fill in your own expense categories.

Income Record how much you make monthly. List all sources of income.		Expenses Record your monthly expenses.
	Rent or mortgage	
	Utilities	
	Insurance	
	Childcare	
	Auto	
	Grocery	
	Fuel	

Total Income: _____

Total Expenses: _____

Budgeting is super important. You don't want to live paycheck to paycheck, but let's face it, Hawaii is expensive. If you can live below your means, be frugal, and avoid buying flashy things—like that gold chain or a Toyota Tacoma with $10,000 rims—you can invest that money instead. If you feel your total expenses are too high, now is a great time to go through and eliminate things from your expenses that you're willing to do without while you grow. Now subtract

your total expenses from your total income and determine what portion of the remainder you'll have to work with every month. And hey, if that number comes up negative—don't panic. That just means it's time to hustle a little harder: pick up a side gig, sell some stuff you don't need, or find a way to bring in extra income while you trim excess spending.

Total Available for Investing Monthly: _____

Step 3: Improve Your Credit Score

The total amount available from your personal resources for investing isn't your only funding source for deals. If you need to, refer back to the funding strategies in chapter 7.7. And when it comes to getting a funder, there's something you can start working on right now that will help you qualify for funding: your credit score.

First, it's important to monitor your credit score. You can do that for free online at Credit Karma. Make sure your credit reports are accurate and dispute any unknown charges. If you spot charges or accounts you don't recognize, don't wait—contact the creditor and file a dispute right away. Cleaning that stuff up now can make a big difference when it's time to sit down with a lender. Another good rule of thumb is to keep your debt balances below 30% of your total credit available. If you've got outstanding debts, start by tackling the smallest ones first—it builds momentum and frees up monthly cash flow that can be applied to your first real estate deals.

Enter your current credit score below or in the Getting Started Guide:

My Credit Score: _____

Step 4: Choose a Real Estate Investing Strategy

Once I had everything in order with my credit and finances, I looked at the different real estate investing strategies. (If you need a refresher on real estate investing strategies, flip back to chapter 7.2.) The most realistic strategies for me at the time were fix-and-flip or wholesaling. Both strategies would help me create some immediate active income that I could then roll into new deals and projects.

Now, when I make a profit from deals, I use that money to pay off debts and then look for opportunities to reinvest. Whether it's a new build, a fixer-upper, or a rental property, I'm always looking to make my money work for me. Eventually, I worked to acquire multiple rental properties that now generate enough income for me to retire on. If I stopped working today, my family could live off that rental income.

Now it's your turn. Which real estate investing strategy or strategies will you start with? Check or circle the real estate strategy of your choice here or in the Getting Started Guide.

- Fix-and-Flip
- Wholesaling
- New Builds
- Rental Properties
- Commercial Properties

Once you set your first real estate and life goals, and get your finances and credit score sorted out, you're ready to dive into your first real estate deal. Congratulations! With the entire

HUI Framework that you've read inside this book, you know exactly what to do every step of the journey.

In the next chapter, you'll find my favorite resources for Hawaii real estate investors. You'll find links to websites on business formation, taxes, leasehold properties, and more!

Chapter 11

Resources for Hawaii Real Estate Investors

In this chapter, you'll find information about the resources mentioned in this book—all organized by chapter.

INTRODUCTION RESOURCES

HUI Academy and Mastermind – A real estate investment course and mastermind program founded by me (Fuzzy Jardine) and my business partner, Zasha Smith. It focuses on mentorship and community support for investors. *https://huimastermind.com/*

Chapter 3 Resources

Hawaiian Community Assets – A nonprofit organization offering free financial education and information on grants and loans to help Hawaiians build generational wealth. *https://hawaiiancommunity.net/*

Hawai'i Community Lending – Another nonprofit that provides loans to local businesses and connects people with federal grants and non-profit funds. *https:// hawaiicommunitylending.com/*

101 Financial – Provides paid financial counseling and financial resources for Hawaiians. Their website offers a digital version of *The Super Duper Simple Book on Money* by Alan Akina. *https://www.superdupersimplebooks.com/*

CHAPTER 6 RESOURCES

Recommended Reading:
Rich Dad Poor Dad by Robert Kiyosaki

Napoleon Hill's Keys to Success by Napoleon Hill

Awaken the Giant Within by Tony Robbins

How to Win Friends and Influence People by Dale Carnegie

The Miracle Morning by Hal Elrod

Atomic Habits by James Clear

The E-Myth Revisited by Michael E. Gerber

The E-Myth Real Estate Investor by Michael E. Gerber, Than Merril and Paul Esajian

CHAPTER 7 RESOURCES

In this chapter, I shared links to some of the resources my business partner, Zasha, and I have used to set up our businesses. These are recommendations based on what we've used. We do not earn any affiliate income from these entities.

Horizon Trust – A self-directed custodial account that allows you to control your 401K yourself.

LegalZoom – You can use LegalZoom to create contracts and agreements, for an LLC, and more. *https://www.legalzoom.com/*

Nevada Corporate Headquarters – You can also use Nevada Corporate Headquarters to form your LLC and keep your identity protected inside your business. *https://nchinc.com/*

Prime Corporate Services – Prime Corporate Services can help with business formation, tax and financial strategies, and business funding and credit services. *https://www.primecorporateservices.com/*

Pyramid INS – Pyramid Insurance offers customers a wide range of property and casualty insurance. *https://www.pyramidins.com/*

Department of Commerce and Consumer Affairs – This office investigates complaints of fraudulent and unfair business practices. When you're looking for contractors, the Department of Commerce and Consumer Affairs is a great place to find contacts. *https://hdcca.hawaii.gov/s/*

Bureau of Conveyances – Access land documents and find out who holds property titles. https://dlnr.hawaii.gov/boc/

Hawaii's Owner-Builder Guide – If you're planning to act as your own contractor, make sure you stay compliant with all of Hawaii's owner-builder laws and regulations by downloading this document. *https://cca.hawaii.gov/rico/files/2019/08/CLB-190718-CLB-Owner-Builder.pdf*

Hawaii Life Blog on Owner-Builder Issues – For more information on Hawaii Owner-Builder regulations, visit *https://www.hawaiilife.com/blog/owner-builder-issues/*

CHAPTER 9 RESOURCES

Department of Hawaiian Home Lands – To identify leasehold properties in Hawaii. *https://dhhl.hawaii.gov/dhhl/*

Hawaii County Lava Zone Maps – Check which lava zone a piece of property is on. *https://files.hawaii.gov/dbedt/op/gis/maps/vhzones_map.pdf*

Hawaii Coastal Erosion Maps – Estimate whether a property is in danger of coastal erosion. *https://opendata.hawaii.gov/dataset/fa-i-erosion-maps*

Hawaii County Tax Auctions – View a list of upcoming tax auctions. *https://www.hawaiipropertytax.com/taxsale.html*

Hawaii Department of Taxation – For information about your tax obligations as a property owner, visit the Hawaiian Department of Taxation website. *https://tax.hawaii.gov/*

CHAPTER 10 RESOURCES

HUI Getting Started Guide – visit *https://huimastermind.com/case-study-step1-page* to download the printable guide.

CONCLUSION

Here we are at the end of the book—but really, this is just the beginning. When you first picked up this book, maybe you were curious, maybe you were searching for a way to build wealth, or maybe, like so many Hawaiians, you were looking for a way to come back home without getting buried by the cost of living.

Whatever got you here, I hope by now you see that real estate investing isn't just for the lucky few. It's for anyone willing to learn, take action, and do things the Pono Way. This isn't just about making money. It's about creating a future where Hawaiians don't have to leave their homeland just to survive.

Now, it's your move.

Are you going to keep waiting or will you be the crab that finally makes it out of the bucket—refusing to let any of the other crabs pull you back down? I've given you the roadmap to get started in this book. And to help you remember everything you've learned during our time together, here's what we've covered:

Hawaiians Are Being Priced Out of Paradise

Hawaiians are leaving their homeland in record numbers because they can't afford to stay. Real estate prices are soaring, and outside investors are snatching up properties, driving up taxes, and leaving locals with few options. This book is about changing that and empowering Hawaiians to reclaim ownership in a way that's ethical, profitable, and sustainable.

From Prison to Property Investor—If I Can Do It, So Can You

My path wasn't a straight one. I spent time in prison, worked multiple jobs just to survive, and nearly fell into the trap of thinking my future was set in stone. But one day, I heard an ad for real estate investing on the radio, and that moment changed my life. I didn't have money, experience, or connections, but I did have determination. I tipped the bucket and climbed out, and if I can do it, you can, too.

The Pono Way to Invest with Heart

If you're going to invest in real estate in Hawaii, do it ethically. Real estate investing in Hawaii isn't just about making money—it's about doing what's right. That's what the Pono Way is all about. It's investing in a way that respects the land, honors our culture, and creates opportunities for locals instead of pushing them out.

This isn't just a business strategy. It's a mission.

Your Step-by-Step Guide to Investing in Hawaii Real Estate

Success isn't about luck. It's about following a system. The HUI Framework teaches you exactly how to find, analyze, and fund properties using other people's money and time. From setting up your business to managing projects, I break down the process so you can start building wealth the right way—the Pono Way.

You Don't Need Your Own Money to Get Started

The biggest myth in real estate investing is that you need money to make money. Wrong. I started with nothing and learned how to leverage other people's money to buy, renovate, and sell properties for a profit. Whether it's using credit, partnering with investors, or tapping into creative financing options, this book shows you how to get started with other people's money.

Building Trust is Everything in Hawaii Real Estate

Hawaiians are skeptical of investors, and for good reason. Too many outsiders have taken advantage of our people. If you want to succeed, you need to earn trust. That means leading by building relationships, respecting the land, and proving that you're in Hawaii to help, not just to profit.

Overcoming the Crab-in-the-Bucket Mentality

What is the hardest part of chasing success? The people around you might not get it. Maybe they'll call you "high maka maka"—someone who thinks they're better than everyone else—but you can't let that stop you. Breaking out of the cycle you're in means doing things differently, and sometimes that means being the first person in your family or social group to make a change.

Know the Rules of Hawaii Real Estate Before You Invest

Investing in Hawaii isn't like investing on the mainland. We have leasehold properties, kuleana lands, and unique property laws that you will need to understand before you make a move. This book breaks it all down so you don't make costly mistakes.

Real Estate Investing Can Help Bring Hawaiians Home
Too many of our people have been forced to leave the islands just to survive. By investing the Pono Way, we can create affordable housing, help locals stay in their homes, and build generational wealth so Hawaiians can thrive in their homeland.

Lift Others Up as You Succeed
The greatest success isn't just making money—it's helping others do the same. That's why I started the HUI Mastermind where I mentor Hawaiians and mainlanders who want to invest in real estate in Hawaii, the Pono Way. When we invest with heart, everyone wins.

YOUR FUTURE IS CALLING

Imagine what your life could look like as someone who invests in Hawaii real estate. You wake up in the morning, but instead of rushing to punch a clock or sitting in traffic for hours, you step outside onto your own land, breathing in the island air, knowing that *your time belongs to you.* Maybe you're working on a new investment deal, maybe you're spending the day with your family, or maybe you're mentoring another Hawaiian who's ready to make their own way out of the bucket.

Now picture what life would look like with more Pono real estate investors on an even bigger scale. More Hawaiians could stay *in* Hawaii instead of being forced out because they can't afford to live here anymore. More families could pass their property and homes down to future generations, instead of just their memories. Land would be developed in a way that respects culture and tradition—not just profit margins. This is what real estate investing the Pono Way can do.

For you, real estate investing means financial freedom. It means no more grinding away at multiple jobs just to scrape by. It means having the power to choose how you spend your days, the resources to care for your family, and the ability to create a legacy that outlives you. It's not just about money—it's about control, *ownership*, and knowing that you're building something that will stand the test of time.

For Hawaii, ethical investing means *we get to stay home.* It means more Hawaiians owning land instead of watching outsiders buy it all up. It means keeping our culture, our traditions, and our *ohana* strong. It means *we* decide what happens to our land—not big developers, not foreign investors, but *us.*

The choice is yours. You can stay where you are, or you can take that first step, climb out of the bucket, and start building a future that's yours. A future where your time is your own, your wealth is growing, and your success is helping keep Hawaiians in their homeland.

WHAT TO DO NEXT

This book is more than a guide to making money in real estate. It's a call to action. It's about breaking cycles, taking control of your future, and investing in ways that create a lasting impact for Hawaii and its people.

Are you looking for help getting started? Want a community where you can plug in, ask questions, and get live feedback and coaching? Then HUI Academy and Mastermind might be for you! Visit https://huimastermind. com/contact-us to book a call with the team, and we will help you figure out your best next step. Let's get to work.

Aloha,

Fuzzy

RESOURCES

Introduction

1 Brittany Rico, Joyce Key Hahn, and Paul Jacobs, "Chuukese and Papua New Guinean populations fastest growing Pacific Islander groups in 2020. Census.gov. (2023, November 1). https://www.census.gov/library/stories/2023/09/2020-census-dhc-a-nhpi-population.html.

2 ""New census data confirms more Native Hawaiians reside on the continent than in Hawai'i." Office of Hawaiian Affairs. (2023, September 25). Retrieved September 17, 2024. https://www.oha.org/news/new-census-data-more-native-hawaiians-reside-continent/.

3 Adam Yamaguchi and Kerry Breen, *Why Native Hawaiians are being "pushed out of Paradise" in their homeland.* CBS News. (2023, November 4). https://www.cbsnews.com/news/hawaii-native-hawaiians-moving-cost-of-living.

4 Jane Smith, "How much does it cost to buy a house in Hawaii?" *Hawaii Star.* (2023, December 20). https://www.hawaiistar.com/how-much-is-a-house-in-hawaii/.

5 Robin Rothstein, "Examining the cost of living by state in 2024." *Forbes.* (2024, August 27). https://www.forbes.com/advisor/mortgages/cost-of-living-by-state/.

Chapter 1

1 Barclay Palmer, "Key reasons to invest in Real Estate." *Investopedia.* (2022, April 7). https://www.investopedia.com/articles/mortgages-real-estate/11/key-reasons-invest-real-estate.asp.

2 Chris Roberts, "Council post: Eight reasons you should consider real estate investing." *Forbes.* (2024, August 12). https://www.forbes.com/councils/forbesrealestatecouncil/2021/02/17/eight-reasons-you-should-consider-real-estate-investing/.

3 Andrew Dehan, "Investment and rental property statistics 2024." *Bankrate.* (2024, August 22). https://www.bankrate.com/mortgages/investment-property-statistics/.

4 Shayna Kusumoto, Jon Yamasato, Andy Arakaki, "9 Reasons to Invest in Hawaii Real Estate." (n.d.) https://realhawaii.co/investors-guide.

5 Samuel Stebbins, "How the foreclosure rate in Hawaii compares to the Nation." *Hawaii Free Press.* (2022, August 11). https://www.hawaiifreepress. com/Articles-Main/ID/33924/How-the-Foreclosure-Rate-in-Hawaii-Compares-to-the-Nation.

Chapter 2

1 Chelsee Yee, "List: 50 most popular jobs in Hawaii and their wages." KHON 2 *Working for Hawaii.* (2022, June 14). https://www.khon2.com/ local-news/list-50-most-popular-jobs-in-hawaii-and-their-wages/.

2 Jane Smith, "How much does it cost to buy a house in Hawaii?" *Hawaii Star.* (2023, December 20). https://www.hawaiistar.com/how-much-is-a-house-in-hawaii/.

Chapter 7.1

1 https://cca.hawaii.gov/breg/registration/dllc/fees/

Chapter 7.3

1 https://www.investopedia.com/terms/h/hard_money_loan.asp

Chapter 7.5

1 https://www.ziprecruiter.com/Salaries/What-Is-the-Average-Real-Estate-Investor-Salary-by-State

Chapter 7.9

1 https://www.hawaiilife.com/blog/owner-builder-issues/

2 https://cca.hawaii.gov/rico/files/2019/08/CLB-190718-CLB-Owner-Builder.pdf

Chapter 8

1 **LUVA Real Estate.** (n.d.). *Ahupua'a: The Hawaiian Land Division System.* Retrieved December 29, 2024, from https://www.luvarealestate.com/blog/ ahupuaa-the-hawaiian-land-division-system/

2 **Esri StoryMaps.** (n.d.). *Ahupuaʻa: Hawaii's Traditional Land Management System.* Retrieved December 29, 2024, from https://storymaps.arcgis.com/stories/83178f6874b144c98094d298e0a6d749

3 **Aloha 4 All.** (n.d.). *The Ceded Lands.* Retrieved December 29, 2024, from https://aloha4all.org/wordpress/basic-issues/essentials/the-ceded-lands/

Chapter 9

1 Emily VanDerWerff. "Hawaii Sues Homeowner Because His House Fell into the Ocean Despite Efforts to Save It." *New York Post*, 30 Sept. 2024, https://nypost.com/2024/09/30/real-estate/hawaii-sues-homeowner-because-his-house-fell-into-the-ocean-despite-efforts-to-save-it/.

2 "Unlucky Lava? National Parks Still Receive Rock Returns by Mail." *YouTube*, uploaded by KHON2 News, 16 Aug. 2023, https://www.youtube.com/watch?v=xp0JlpgZNbY. Accessed 9 Feb. 2025.

3 "The Legend of Night Marchers in Hawaiʻi." *Hawaii Magazine*, https://www.hawaiimagazine.com/the-legend-of-night-marchers-in-hawaii/. Accessed 9 Feb. 2025.

4 UHERO. *The Hawaii Housing Factbook 2024.* University of Hawaiʻi Economic Research Organization, 2024, https://uhero.hawaii.edu/the-hawaii-housing-factbook-2024/. Accessed 9 Feb. 2025.

5 Nolo. *What Happens If I Don't Pay Property Taxes in Hawaii?* Nolo, https://www.nolo.com/legal-encyclopedia/what-happens-if-i-don-t-pay-property-taxes-in-hawaii.html.

ABOUT THE AUTHOR

Born and raised in Hawaii, Kolaiah "Fuzzy" Jardine understands the deep connection locals have to the land—and the heartbreak of watching families forced to leave due to rising costs. Determined to be part of the solution, he turned to real estate not just as a career, but as a mission. His goal is to educate and empower local residents with the tools to stay, thrive, and build generational wealth right here at home in Hawaii.

As the cofounder of HUI Mastermind and a mentor to aspiring investors across The Islands, Fuzzy has helped hundreds of locals break the cycle of being priced out of paradise. His passion lies in teaching real estate strategies that actually work for *kamaʻāina* (children of the land)— strategies rooted in community, creativity, and ownership.

Priced Out of Paradise is more than a book. It's a blueprint for hope. For every ohana on the edge of leaving the islands, for every young person wondering if they have a future in Hawaii, this book is a reminder that you don't have to move away to make your life what you want it to be. You just need the right knowledge, the right mindset, and the right support.

www.ingramcontent.com/pod-product-compliance
Lightning Source LLC
Chambersburg PA
CBHW071337210326
41597CB00015B/1475